POCKET

BUDAPEST

T ... NCES

NORWAY
Murmansk
FINLAND
Gulf of Finland
SWEDEN
RUSSIA
ESTONIA
Moscow
LATVIA
Baltic Sea
LITH.
Kaliningrad
BELARUS
GERMANY
POLAND
Kyiv
UKRAINE
CZECH REP.
CRIMEA
HUNGARY
ROMANIA
Black Sea
ITALY
BULGARIA
NATO members
TURKEY

Contents

Plan Your Trip 4

Matthias Church (p42), Castle District

Explore Budapest 31

Worth a Trip

Survival Guide 145

Special Features

Welcome to Budapest

Straddling the Danube with the Buda Hills as backdrop and boasting enough baroque, neoclassical and art nouveau architecture to satisfy anyone, Budapest is endowed with both natural and human-created beauty. But the Queen of the Danube is not just a pretty face. At night she dons her party dress to enjoy the region's premier party town.

Széchenyi Chain Bridge (p97) across the Danube River
ZSOLT HLINKA / GETTY IMAGES ©

Top Sights

Royal Palace

Seat of power for centuries. p34

TIBOR BOGNAR / GETTY IMAGES ©

ATLANTIDE PHOTOTRAVEL / GETTY IMAGES ©

Gellért Baths

Like bathing in a cathedral. **p52**

JIRI SEBESTA / SHUTTERSTOCK ©

Basilica of St Stephen

Hungary's most sacred church and relic. **p92**

INGOLF POMPE / LOOK-FOTO / GETTY IMAGES ©

Hungarian National Museum

The nation's most important historical collection. **p130**

Parliament

Hungary's largest and most iconic building. **p90**

PHOTO.UA / SHUTTERSTOCK ©

LEFT: SERGIO DELLE VEDOVE / SHUTTERSTOCK ©; RIGHT: NIGAR ALIZADA / SHUTTERSTOCK ©

Citadella & Liberty Monument

A fortress that never saw battle. **p54**

Memento Park

A kitsch Disneyland of socialist Hungary. **p64**

Aquincum

Well-preserved Roman town. **p74**

City Park

Pest's delightful green lung. **p140**

LEFT: DANITA DELIMONT / GETTY IMAGES ©; RIGHT: VIDALGO / SHUTTERSTOCK ©

FROG DARES / SHUTTERSTOCK ©

Great Synagogue

World's largest synagogue outside NYC. **p112**

Eating

The dining scene in Budapest has undergone a sea change in recent years. Hungarian food has 'lightened up', offering the same wonderfully earthy and spicy tastes but in less calorific dishes. The number of vegetarian (or partially meatless) and even vegan restaurants has increased, and the choice of eateries with cuisines other than Magyar is greater than ever before.

Dining Diversity

A wide choice of ethnic food – from Middle Eastern and Greek to Japanese, Indian, Chinese and even vegetarian, has become almost the norm in Budapest. And the fast food of choice in the capital is no longer cheap-and-cheerful *lángos* (deep-fried dough with various toppings, usually cheese and sour cream), but kebabs and falafel.

Hungarian Cuisine

Gulyás (goulash) is Hungary's signature dish, though here it's more like a soup than a stew and made with beef, onions and tomatoes. Paprika-infused *pörkölt* is closer to what we'd call goulash. *Halászlé* is a highly recommended fish soup made from poached freshwater fish, tomatoes, green peppers and paprika. A popular dessert is *palacsinta*, a crêpe filled with jam, sweet cheese or chocolate sauce.

Best Traditional Hungarian

Kádár Étkezde Lunch-only *étkezde* (canteen) on an atmospheric square. (p122)

Földes Józsi Konyhája Excellent Hungarian home-style dishes. (p73)

Best Modern Hungarian

Mák Bisztró Inventive Hungarian dishes from a daily-changing blackboard. (p98)

21 Magyar Vendéglő Fine Hungarian dining in the Castle District. (p45)

ESCA Studio New modern Hungarian bistro offering superb value. (p122)

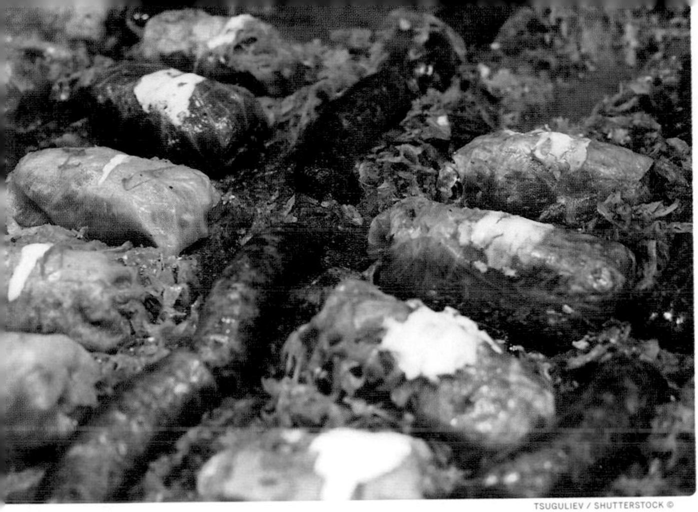

Best Italian & Mediterranean

Babka Hip go-to spot for inspired Mediterranean dishes. (p107)

Marcello This simple Italian place has been a student favourite for two decades. (p59)

Pizzica Quite simply the best real Italian pizza in town. (p97)

Best Fish & Seafood

Horgásztanya Vendéglő Reliable Hungarian fish dishes by the Danube. (p45)

bigfish Super-fresh fish and shellfish. (p98)

Halkakas Halbistró Fresh, simple and good-value fish dishes. (p124)

Best for Breakfast

Kőleves Breakfast spot with good vegetarian choices. (p124)

Centrál Kávéház Traditional cafe with a terrace for sunny mornings. (p86)

Sarki Fűszeres Retro-style cafe on a tree-lined street perfect for brunch. (p107)

Top Tip

If you're on a buget, eat your main meal at lunchtime; set meals at lunch at most restaurants – including high-end ones – cost a fraction of what they do at dinnertime.

Drinking & Nightlife

In recent years Budapest has justifiably gained a reputation as one of Europe's leading nightlife destinations. Alongside its age-old cafe culture, it offers a magical blend of unique drinking holes, fantastic wine, home-grown firewaters and emerging craft beers, all served up with a warm Hungarian welcome and a wonderful sense of fun.

What to Drink Where

If you want to sample the local beer (most commonly Dreher, Kőbányai and Arany Ászok), head for a *söröző*, a 'pub' with *csapolt sör* (draught beer) served in a *pohár* (0.3L glass) or *korsó* (0.4L or 0.5L glass). A *borozó* or *bor pince* is a traditional establishment (usually a dive) serving wine. Modern wine bars serve wine by the *deci* (decilitre, 0.1L) so you can sample a wide range.

Cafes

The *kávéház* (cafe) has long been an integral part of Budapest's social life, and old-style cafes, some of which date back as much as a century and a half, abound in Budapest. The new breed of coffee house roasts its own blends and imports specific beans.

Ruin Pubs & Garden Clubs

Unique to Budapest, *romkocsmák* (ruin pubs) began to appear in the city in the early 2000s when abandoned buildings were turned into pop-up bars. At the same time, during the city's long and very hot summers, so-called *kertek* (literally 'gardens' but here any outdoor entertainment zone) empty out even the most popular indoor bars and clubs.

Best Wine & Cocktail Bars

Doblo Romantic brick-lined bar with a huge variety of Hungarian wine. (p125)

Oscar American Bar Film decor and cool cocktails below the castle. (p47)

DiVino Borbár Come here to taste your way through Hungary's wine regions. (p99)

LUMOKAJLINIOJ / SHUTTERSTOCK ©

Best Garden Clubs & Ruin Bars

Instant Multilevel venue with a bar for every taste. (p126)

Élesztő High-quality craft beer, and lots of it. (p139)

Szimpla Kert Budapest's first and most popular *romkocsma*. (pictured; p125)

Best Traditional Cafes

Művész Kávéház People-watch with the Hungarian State Opera House as backdrop. (p126)

Gerbeaud Serving impeccable cakes and coffee since 1858. (p81)

Ruszwurm Cukrászda The oldest traditional cafe in town. (p47)

Best Rooftop Bars

High Note Roof Bar Major 'wow' factor above the Aria Hotel. (p99)

Leo Budapest His Highness Leo takes in views over Castle Hill and the Danube in Buda. (p45)

Top Tip

Pest's two main nightlife strips are trendy VI Liszt Ferenc tér, where you'll have to fight for a spot under the plane trees, and IX Ráday utca, a more subdued pedestrianised street in Józsefváros full of pubs, bars and modern cafes. Up and coming is V Szent István tér around the basilica.

Shopping

Budapest is a fantastic city for shopping, whether you're in the market for traditional folk craft, cutting-edge designer goods, the latest in flash headgear or honey-sweet dessert wine. Traditional markets stand side by side with mammoth shopping malls, and old-style umbrella-makers can still be found next to avant-garde fashion boutiques.

Specialities & Souvenirs

Traditional items with a Hungarian brand – called Hungarica here – include folk embroidery and ceramics, pottery, wall hangings, painted wooden toys and boxes, dolls, all types of basketry, and porcelain (especially that from Herend and Zsolnay). Feather or goose-down pillows and duvets (comforters) are of exceptionally high quality.

Foodstuffs that are expensive or difficult to buy elsewhere – goose liver (both fresh and potted), dried mushrooms, jam (especially apricot), prepared meats like Pick salami, the many types of paprika – make nice gifts (as long as you're allowed to take them into your country). Hungary's 'boutique' wines also make excellent gifts; a bottle of *six-puttonyos* (the sweetest) Tokaji Aszú dessert wine always goes down a treat.

Markets

Some people consider a visit to one of Budapest's markets a highlight, not just as a place to indulge their consumer vices but also as the consummate Budapest experience. The city counts 20 markets, with most of them in Pest. The vast majority are closed on Sunday, and Monday is always very quiet, with only a few stalls open.

Best for Hungarica

Herend Finest Hungarian porcelain is the ultimate gift or souvenir. (p49)

Memories of Hungary Museum-quality souvenirs a step from the basilica. (p101)

Holló Műhely Atelier/shop selling attractive folk art with a modern look. (p87)

Best for Food & Drink

Nagycsarnok Huge market hall selling everything from fruit and veg to paprika and goose liver. (pictured; p133)

Bortársaság The first port of call for buying most wines. (p49)

Magyar Pálinka Háza Shelves and shelves of all kinds of *pálinka* (fruit brandy). (p139)

Best for Books

Bestsellers Budapest's most complete English-language bookshop; helpful staff. (p101)

Massolit Books & Cafe New and second-hand books in an atmospheric old shop with a little garden. (p127)

Központi Antikvárium The largest and oldest antique bookshop in Eastern Europe. (p133)

Best for Clothing

Vass Shoes Classic footwear – cobbled for you or ready to wear. (p87)

Pannon Glove High-fashion and leather gloves. (p87)

Szputnyik Shop D-20 Shop stuffed with vintage and alternative fashion. (p127)

Shopping Streets

Antiques V Falk Miksa utca in Pest and II Frankel Leó út in Buda.

Antiquarian & secondhand books V Múzeum körút in Pest.

Fashion & souvenirs V Váci utca in Pest.

International brands V Deák Ferenc utca (Fashion St) in Pest.

Local designer goods VI Király utca in Pest.

Tours

If you can't be bothered making your own way around Budapest or don't have the time, a guided tour can be a great way to learn the lie of the land.

Best Walking Tours

Walking tours are run by various companies, and most tend to be standard three-hour jaunts that take in the city's main attractions.

Free Budapest Tours (www.freebudapesttours.eu) Innovative walking tours organised by an outfit whose guides work for tips only, so dig deep. The three-hour tour of Budapest's top sights in English departs from in front of the Basilica of St Stephen on V Szent István tér daily at 10.30am and 2.30pm.

Absolute Walking Tours (www.absolutetours.com) A 3½-hour guided walk of City Park, central Pest, past Parliament (pictured) and around Castle Hill with a cafe stop. Run by the people behind Yellow Zebra Bikes. Tours depart daily from the Absolute Tours Centre behind the Hungarian State Opera House.

Best Bus Tours

Hugely popular are hop-on, hop-off bus tours that allow you to board and alight as you please for a selected length of time.

Program Centrum (www.programcentrum.hu) This company's Budapest sightseeing tours include tickets valid for 48 hours for two bus routes (one taped in 16 languages, one with live commentary in English), a one-hour river cruise and a walking tour.

Cityrama Gray Line (www.cityrama.hu) If you prefer to stay on a bus without hopping on and off, this operator has three-hour tours with three photo stops and commentary in five languages.

Best Cycling Tours

Most bike-hire outfits offer tours for around 8000Ft per person, but itineraries can depend on the whim of the group leader.

Yellow Zebra Bikes (www.yellowzebrabikes.com) Tours take in Heroes' Sq, City Park and central Pest in four hours, departing daily at 11am from April to October and Wednesday, Friday, Saturday and Sunday only in March and November.

JOHN DAKERS / GETTY IMAGES ©

Budapest Bike (www.budapestbike.hu) Offers some of the best bike tours in Budapest, including a three-hour coffee and market tour (12,000Ft) and a five-hour jaunt to Szentendre (11,000Ft) on the Danube Bend.

Best Boat Tours

A slew of companies offer cruises on the Danube that include taped commentary in a multitude of languages and (usually) a free drink. Most boats depart from the piers between Széchenyi Chain and Elizabeth bridges, especially Vigadó tér Pier.

Mahart PassNave (www.mahartpassnave.hu) One-hour cruises along the Danube on the hour from 10am to 9pm, plus at 10pm in July and August. Taped commentary in a dozen languages.

River Ride (www.riverride.com) Bright-yellow amphibious bus takes you on a two-hour tour of Budapest by road and river; live commentary in English and German (recorded in many other languages).

Best Special Interest Tours

Some outfits run specialised tours. Some combine driving and walking, while others are only walking; themes include Jewish history, contemporary art, art nouveau, nightlife and more.

Jewish Heritage Tours (www.ticket.info.hu) Recommended tours delve into the culture and history of Budapest's Jewish community.

Top Tip

The **Budapest Card** (www.budapestinfo.hu) includes two free guided walking tours and offers discounts on other tours too.

Thermal Baths & Pools

Budapest lies on the geological fault separating the Buda Hills from the Great Plain, and more than 30,000 cu metres of warm to scalding (21°C to 76°C) mineral water gush forth daily from some 123 thermal and more than 400 mineral springs. As a result, the city is a major spa centre, and 'taking the waters' is a true Budapest experience.

What's Inside

The layout of most of Budapest's baths – both old and new – follows a similar pattern: a series of indoor thermal pools, where temperatures range from warm to hot, with steam rooms, saunas, ice-cold plunge pools and rooms for massage. Some have outdoor pools with fountains, wave machines and whirlpools.

Getting In & Out

The procedure for getting out of your street clothes and into the water requires some explanation. All baths and pools have cabins or lockers. In most of the baths nowadays you are given an electronic bracelet that directs you to, and then opens, your locker or cabin. Ask for assistance if you can't work it out.

What to Bring

Fewer and fewer baths have male- and female-only days, so pack a bathing suit or be prepared to rent one (around 1500Ft). Some pools require the use of a bathing cap; bring your own or wear the disposable ones provided or sold from 200Ft. You might also consider taking along a pair of plastic sandals.

UNGVARI ATTILA / SHUTTERSTOCK ©

Choosing a Bath

Rudas Baths These renovated baths, built in 1566, are the most Turkish of all in Budapest. They're mostly men-only during the week but mixed on weekend nights. (p58)

Gellért Baths Soaking in these art nouveau baths, now open to both men and women at all times, has been likened to taking a bath in a cathedral. The indoor swimming pools are the most beautiful in the city. (p52)

Széchenyi Baths The gigantic 'wedding-cake' building in City Park houses the Széchenyi Baths, which has 15 indoor thermal baths and three outdoor swimming pools. (pictured; p141)

Veli Bej Baths This venerable Turkish bath in Buda dating from 1575 has got a new lease of life after having been forgotten for centuries. (p70)

Király Baths The four small Turkish pools here, while in need of renovation, are the real deal and date back to 1570. (p43)

Top Tips

- Opening times and whether everybody/men/women are welcome depend on the day of the week, but most baths are now completely mixed.
- **Budapest Spas and Hot Springs** (www.spasbudapest.com) has good up-to-date information and allows you to book online.

Entertainment

FERENC SZELEPCSENYI / SHUTTERSTOCK ©

For a city of its size, Budapest has a huge choice of things to do and places to go after dark, from opera and folk dancing to live jazz and films screened in palatial cinemas. It's usually not difficult getting tickets or getting in; the hard part is deciding what to do and where to go.

Best Classical Music

Liszt Music Academy Budapest's premier venue for classical concerts amidst wonderful Zsolnay porcelain and frescoes. (p120)

Palace of Arts The city's most up-to-date cultural venue with two concert halls and near-perfect acoustics. (pictured; p139)

Hungarian State Opera House Small but perfectly formed home to both the state opera company and the Hungarian National Ballet. (p96)

Best Live Music

Akvárium Klub In an old bus terminal, three venues serve up a quality line-up of live acts. (p87)

Gödör Klub Great gigs in the midst of banging Erzsébetváros. (p126)

La Bodeguita del Medio Great venue for live Cuban music nightly. (p123)

Best Jazz & Blues

Budapest Jazz Club Very sophisticated club for traditional, vocal and Latin jazz. (p109)

Jedermann Cafe Relaxed Ráday utca hang-out for lunch, grills and great jazz. (p133)

Top Tips

- Consult the listings in **Funzine** (www.funzine.hu) and **PestiEst** (www.est.hu).
- Handy websites for booking theatre and concert tickets include www.jegymester.hu. and www.kulturinfo.hu.

Museums & Galleries

Unlike most other European cities, Budapest does not have a single museum founded from a royal treasury. Instead, support came from an increasingly politicised aristocracy, which saw the value of safeguarding the nation's relics and artwork. Today the city counts some five dozen museums devoted to subjects as diverse as op art, musical instruments, trade and tourism, and folk costume.

PETER CSASZAR / SHUTTERSTOCK ©

Best History Museums

Aquincum Museum Excellent museum with collection of Roman finds. (p74)

Castle Museum Renovated museum walks you through Budapest history. (p35)

House of Terror Focuses on the atrocities of fascist and Stalinist regimes. (p120)

Best Art Museums

Vasarely Museum Devoted to wacky op art. (p70)

Museum of Fine Arts Houses Budapest's most outstanding collection of foreign artworks. (pictured; p141)

Hungarian National Gallery Home to the most important Hungarian art. (p35)

Best Cultural Museums

Music History Museum Filled with scores and musical instruments. (p42)

Hungarian Museum of Trade & Tourism The catering and hospitality trade through objects and advertising. (p70)

House of Houdini Life of locally born illusionist and escape artist. (p43)

Top Tips

- Wear comfortable shoes and make use of the cloakrooms.
- Limit yourself: choose a particular period or section and pretend that everything else is elsewhere.

For Kids

Budapest abounds in places that will delight children, and there is always a special child's entry rate (and often a family one as well) to fee-paying attractions. Visits to many areas of the city can be designed around a rest stop or picnic – at City Park, say, or on Margaret Island.

ZOLTÁN MAX / EYEEM / GETTY IMAGES ©

Best Museums & Galleries

Museum of Fine Arts Program allows kids to handle original Egyptian artefacts and create their own masterpieces of art. (p141)

Aquincum Museum Great interactive exhibits including virtual duelling with a gladiator. (p74)

Budapest Zoo World-class collection of big cats, hippopotamuses, polar bears and giraffes. (pictured; p142)

Gellért Baths An abundance of outdoor and indoor pools; the outdoor one has a wave machine. (p52)

Budavár Cultural Centre Regularly scheduled kids' *táncház* (folk music and dance) weekends. (p49)

Best Public Transport

Sikló Climbing up to Castle Hill at an angle. (p39)

Cog Railway This unusual conveyance will delight kids. (p77)

Children's Railway Kids in charge in the Buda Hills. (p77)

Best Entertainment

Budapest Puppet Theatre Kids will be transfixed by the marionette shows even if they don't speak Hungarian. (p127)

Top Tips

- Most restaurants won't have a set children's menu but will usually split the adult serving.
- Budapest's traditional cafes and *cukrászdák* (cake shops) will satisfy a sweet tooth of any size.

LGBT

Budapest offers a reasonable gay scene for its size. Most gay people are discreet in public places and displays of affection are rare. Lesbian social life remains very much underground, with lots of private parties. Attitudes are changing, but society generally remains conservative on this issue.

ZKK600 / GETTY IMAGES ©

Best Clubs

Alterego Still the city's premier gay club (and don't you forget it) with the best dance music. (p100)

Best Bars

CoXx Men's Bar Cruising city, with huge bar and some large areas out the back. (p126)

Tuk Tuk Bar Relaxed, Asian theme cocktail bar with very friendly staff. (p125)

Best Accommodation

Casati Budapest Hotel Tasteful conversion in the centre of Pest with cool decor and funky covered courtyard. (p147)

Best Festivals

Budapest Pride This week-long gay, lesbian, bisexual and transgender film and cultural festival (pictured; www.budapestpride.com) culminates in the annual Pride Parade, usually held on the first Saturday in July.

Useful Resources

Budapest GayGuide (www.budapest.gayguide.net) Good listings and insider advice.

Háttér Society (Háttér Társaság; ☎1-329 2670; www.hatter.hu) Information and Counselling Hotline (☎1-329 3380) open 6pm to 11pm daily.

Labrisz (www.labrisz.hu) Info on the city's lesbian scene.

Four Perfect Days

Day 1

PFEIFFER / SHUTTERSTOCK ©

Spend your first morning on Castle Hill, taking in the views from the **Royal Palace** (p34). There are museums aplenty up here, but choose either the **Hungarian National Gallery** (p35) for Hungarian fine art or the **Castle Museum** (p35) for a seamless introduction to the city's tortuous past.

In the afternoon take the **Sikló** (funicular, pictured; p39) down to Clark Ádám tér and walk up Fő utca to the **Király Baths** (p43) for a nice soak.

Depending on your mood, check to see what's on in the way of *táncház* (folk music and dance) at the **Budavár Cultural Centre** (p49) below Castle Hill or head for **Oscar American Bar** (p47) south of the square for cocktails and music.

Day 2

GOODLIFESTUDIO / GETTY IMAGES ©

The next day cross the Danube and see Pest at its very finest by walking up leafy **Andrássy út** (p120) to **Heroes' Square** (pictured; p141), taking you past the delightful **Hungarian State Opera House** (p96) and such wonderful cafes as **Művész Kávéház** (p126).

As you approach City Park, decide whether you want an educational or leisurely afternoon. The **House of Terror** (p120) is on Andrássy út and on the northern side of Heroes' Sq is the renovated **Museum of Fine Arts** (p141). City Park contains the **Budapest Zoo** (p142) and the wonderful **Széchenyi Baths** (p141).

In the evening, head back down Andrássy út to Erzsébetváros and have drinks at **La Bodeguita del Medio** (p123).

Day 3

SPUMADOR / SHUTTERSTOCK ©

On day three, first concentrate on the two icons of Hungarian nationhood: the Crown of St Stephen in the **Parliament** (p90) building and the saint-king's mortal remains (just a hand) in the **Basilica of St Stephen** (p92).

In the afternoon, concentrate on the Jewish Quarter, with a neighbourhood walk taking in such sights as Klauzál tér, the **Orthodox Synagogue** (pictured; p121) and the original ghetto wall. Make sure you leave ample time for a good look inside the **Great Synagogue** (p112) and its **Hungarian Jewish Museum** (p113).

In the evening move on to the *kertek* ('garden clubs') within along Kazinczy utca, including the granddaddy of them all, **Szimpla Kert** (p125).

Day 4

PELLE ZOLTAN / SHUTTERSTOCK ©

On your last day, stroll through atmospheric Óbuda and learn how Buda, Óbuda and Pest all came together. The **Vasarely Museum** (p70) and its hallucinogenic op art always pleases and the nearby **Hungarian Museum of Trade & Tourism** (p70) is delightful. Alternatively, **Aquincum** (p74) is just a vert short HÉV train ride away.

In the afternoon, head for **Margaret Bridge** (p105). Just up the hill is **Gül Baba's Tomb** (pictured; p71), the only Muslim place of pilgrimage in northern Europe. Then pamper yourself at **Veli Bej Baths** (p70).

At night cross over Margaret Bridge to Újlipótváros and the **Budapest Jazz Club** (p109), the most serious such venue in town.

Need to Know

For detailed information, see Survival Guide (p145)

Currency
Forint (Ft)

Language
Hungarian

Visas
Generally not required for stays up to 90 days.

Money
ATMs are everywhere, including at the airport, and train and bus stations. Visa, MasterCard and American Express are widely accepted.

Mobile Phones
Local SIM cards can be used in European and Australian phones, as well as most North American ones. Roaming fees are not applied on EU phones when used here.

Time
Central European Time (GMT/UTC plus one hour)

Tipping
Nearly everyone in Budapest routinely tips waiters, hairdressers and taxi drivers.

Daily Budget

Budget: Less than 15,000Ft
Dorm bed: 3000–6500Ft

Meal at self-service restaurant: 1500–2500Ft

Three-day transport pass: 4150Ft

Midrange: 15,000–35,000Ft
Single/double private room: from 7500/10,000Ft

Two-course meal with drink: 3500–7500Ft

Cocktail: from 1500Ft

Top End: More than 35,000Ft
Double room in superior hotel: from 16,500Ft

Dinner for two with wine at good restaurant: from 12,500Ft

All-inclusive ticket at a spa: adult/child 3600/1600Ft

Cover charge at a popular club: 1500–2500Ft

Advance Planning

Two months before If travelling in high season or during big festivals, book your accommodation; reserve a table at a top restaurant.

One month before Check listings in the Budapest Events Guide (www.budapesteventsguide.com) and Budapest Times (www.budapesttimes.hu); book popular events.

One week before Call your bank/credit-card company to tell them you're travelling and ask about 'contactless payment'. It's very common here.

Arriving in Budapest

Most people arrive in Budapest by air, but you can also get here from dozens of European cities by bus or train.

Ferenc Liszt International Airport

Minibuses, buses and trains to central Budapest run from 4.30am to 11.50pm (700Ft to 2000Ft); taxis cost from 6000Ft.

Keleti, Nyugati & Déli Train Stations

All three stations are connected to metro lines of the same name; night buses serve them when the metro closes.

Népliget & Stadion Bus Stations

Both bus stations are on metro lines (M3 and M2 respectively) and are served by tram 1.

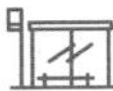

Getting Around

Budapest's transport system, run by BKK (www.bkk.hu), is one of the most comprehensive in Europe. Passes on all forms of transport are valid for one day to one month.

Metro

The quickest but least scenic way. Runs 4.30am to about 11.50pm.

Bus

Good network of buses runs from 4.30am to between 9pm and 11.50pm; from 11.50pm to 4.30am a network of 40 night buses kicks in.

Tram

Trams (pictured) are faster and more pleasant for sightseeing than buses. Tram 6 on the Big Ring Road runs overnight.

Taxi

Taxis in Budapest are cheap by European standards, and are fully regulated.

SUBODH AGNIHOTRI / SHUTTERSTOCK ©

Budapest Neighbourhoods

Óbuda (p67)
This is the oldest part of Buda and retains a lost-in-the-past village feel; here you'll find the remains of the Roman settlement of Aquincum and some legendary eateries.

Castle District (p33)
Castle Hill, nerve centre of Budapest's history and packed with important museums, is here, as is ground-level Víziváros, with some excellent restaurants.

Belváros (p79)
The 'Inner Town' centres on touristy Váci utca, with its shops and bars, and Võrõsmarty tér, home to the city's most celebrated *cukràszda* (cake shop).

Gellért Hill & Tabán (p51)
The Citadella and the Liberty Monument gaze down from atop Gellért Hill in the neighbourhood of Tabán.

Margaret Island & Northern Pest (p103)
This unspoiled island in the Danube offers a green refuge, while northern Pest beckons with its shops and lovely cafes.

Parliament & Around (p89)
Takes in the areas around Parliament building and the equally iconic Basilica of St Stephen, plus Nagymező utca, Budapest's Broadway.

City Park

Erzsébetváros & the Jewish Quarter (p111)
This neighbourhood offers the lion's share of Budapest's accommodation, restaurants serving every cuisine under the sun and the city's hottest nightspots.

Basilica of St Stephen

Great Synagogue

Hungarian National Museum

Gellért Baths

Southern Pest (p129)
Traditionally working class, this is an area to wander, poking your nose into courtyards and small, often traditional, shops.

Explore Budapest

Worth a Trip

Budapest's Walking Tours

Széchenyi Chain Bridge (p97), with view of the Basilica of St Stephen (p92)
YULIYA KHOVBOSHA / SHUTTERSTOCK ©

Explore Castle District

The Castle District encompasses Castle Hill (Várhegy), a 1km-long limestone plateau towering 170m above the Danube. It contains Budapest's most important medieval monuments and museums in two distinct areas: the Old Town and the Royal Palace. Víziváros (Watertown) is the narrow area between the Danube and Castle Hill that spreads as far as Széll Kálmán tér, Buda's most important transport hub.

The Short List

- ***Castle Museum (p35)*** *Enjoying beautifully presented exhibitions in striking surrounds covering 2000 years.*
- ***Hungarian National Gallery (p35)*** *Viewing priceless Gothic wooden sculptures and historical events captured forever by some of the nation's greatest artists.*
- ***Fishermen's Bastion (p42)*** *Taking in views of the Danube and Pest from this faux-medieval landmark.*
- ***Matthias Church (p42)*** *Marvelling at the exquisite tile work of the exterior and climbing the tower for jaw-dropping views.*

Getting There & Around

Bus: V Deák Ferenc tér in Pest for 16 to I Dísz tér on Castle Hill.

Funicular: I Clark Ádám tér for Sikló to I Szent György tér on Castle Hill.

Train: (HÉV) H5 Batthyány tér.

M M2 Batthyány tér & Széll Kálmán tér.

Shuttle Castle Shuttle Budapest.

Castle District Map on p40

Matthias Church (p42) WAKU / SHUTTERSTOCK ©

Top Sight
Royal Palace

Buda's former Royal Palace has been razed and rebuilt many times over the past seven centuries. Béla IV established a royal residence here in the mid-13th century, it was levelled in the battle to drive out the Turks in 1686 and the Habsburgs rebuilt it (but spent very little time here). The palace contains two important museums and the national library.

MAP P40, E8

Királyi Palota

I Szent György tér

16, 16A, 116

Hungarian National Gallery

The **Hungarian National Gallery** (Magyar Nemzeti Galéria; ☎1-201 9082; www.mng.hu; Bldgs A-D; adult/concession 1800/900Ft, audio guide 800Ft; ⏰10am-6pm Tue-Sun) is an overwhelming collection spread across four floors and four wings of the palace that traces Hungarian art from the 11th century to the present day. The largest collections include medieval and Renaissance stonework, Gothic wooden sculptures and panel paintings, and late-Gothic winged altars. The museum also has an important collection of Hungarian paintings and sculpture from the 19th and 20th centuries.

Be advised that the gallery is in a state of flux at present, with the late-Renaissance and baroque art collection moved to the Museum of Fine Arts (p141) in Hősök tere in Pest in preparation for the gallery's future relocation to a new purpose-built museum building in City Park.

The permanent collection is, for the most part, exhibited in Buildings B, C and D, with A and the 3rd floor of all four buildings usually reserved for temporary exhibits.

Castle Museum

The **Castle Museum** (Vármúzeum; ☎1-487 8800; www.btm.hu; Bldg E; adult/concession 2400/1200Ft; ⏰10am-6pm Tue-Sun Mar-Oct, to 4pm Tue-Sun Nov-Feb) explores the city's 2000-year history over four floors. Restored palace rooms dating from the 15th century can be entered from the two-level basement, where there are three vaulted halls. One of the halls features a magnificent Renaissance door frame in red marble bearing the seals of Queen Beatrix and her husband, King Matthias Corvinus, and leading to the Gothic and Renaissance Halls, King's Cellar (1480) and 14th-century Tower Chapel.

★ Top Tips

- The easiest and most fun way to reach Castle Hill is by boarding the Sikló, a funicular railway built in 1870 that ascends from Clark Ádám tér at the western end of Chain Bridge to Szent György tér near the Royal Palace.
- Catch the changing of the guard at Sándor Palace hourly between 9am and 5pm.

✕ Take a Break

If you just want something hot and/or sweet after your visit to the museum(s), head for Ruszwurm Cukrászda (p47) or stop by stylish Pierrot (p46) for a drink in refined surroundings.

On the museum's ground floor, exhibits showcase Budapest during the Middle Ages, with almost 80 important Gothic statues, including heads and fragments of courtiers, squires and saints, that were discovered during excavations in 1974. On the 1st floor, an exhibition called 'Light & Shadow: 1000 Years of a Capital' traces the history of Budapest from the arrival of the Magyars and the Turkish occupation to modern times in 10 multimedia sections, examining housing, ethnic diversity, religion and other issues over the centuries.

National Széchenyi Library

The copyright **National Széchenyi Library** (Országos Széchenyi Könyvtár, OSZK; ☎1-224 3700; www.oszk.hu; Bldg F; ⏲9am-8pm Tue-Sat, stacks to 7pm Tue-Fri, to 5pm Sat) contains codices and manuscripts, a large collection of foreign newspapers and a copy of everything published in Hungary or in the Hungarian language. It was founded in 1802 by Count Ferenc Széchenyi, father of the heroic statesman István, who endowed it with 15,000 books and 2000 manuscripts. This library allows members (daily/monthly 1200/2000Ft) to do research, peruse the general stacks, and read the large collection of foreign newspapers and magazines.

Matthias Fountain

Facing the Royal Palace's large courtyard to the northwest is the Romantic-style **Matthias Fountain** (Mátyás-kút), portraying the young king Matthias Corvinus in hunting garb. To the right below him is Szép Ilona (Beautiful Helen), the protagonist in a Romantic ballad by the poet Mihály Vörösmarty. Apparently, Ilona fell in love with this dashing 'hunter' – who was in reality King Matthias – and, upon learning his true identity and feeling unworthy, died of a broken heart.

Statues & Monuments

To the east of the Habsburg Steps is a bronze statue from 1905 of the **Turul** (Turul szobor), an eagle-like totemic bird that supposedly impregnated Emese, the grandmother of Árpád, the chief military commander who led the Magyar tribes into the Carpathian Basin in about AD 895. To the southeast, just in front of Building C and the main entrance to the Hungarian National Gallery, stands a statue of **Eugene of Savoy** (Savoyai Jenő Műemlék), the Habsburg prince who wiped out the last Turkish army in Hungary at the Battle of Zenta in Serbia in 1697. In the middle of the square on the other side of the building is a statue by György Vastagh of a Hortobágy cowboy *(Hortobágyi csikós)* in full regalia breaking a mighty *bábolna* steed.

Hungarian National Gallery

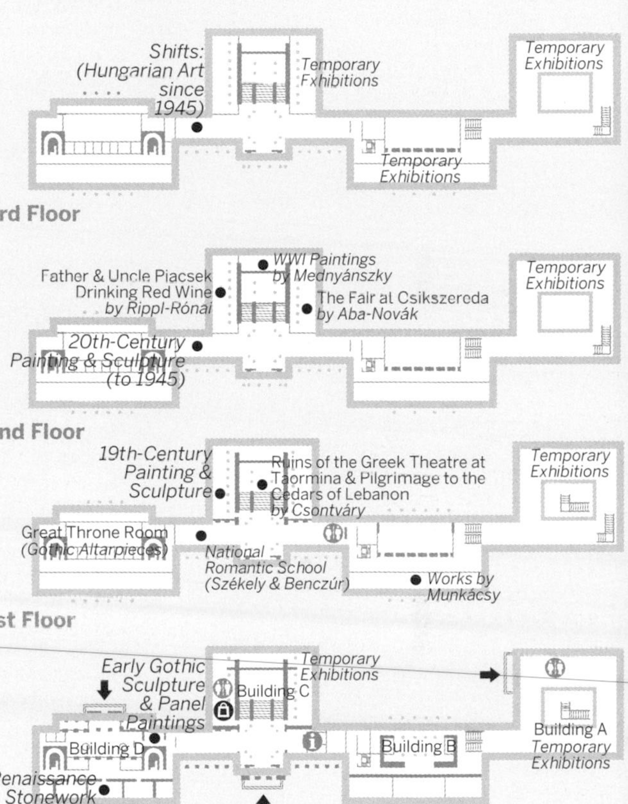

Walking Tour

Castle Hill

There's no better introduction to Budapest than a tour of Castle Hill. The neighbourhood has everything that defines this delightful city: history, architecture, fabulous views and tourists in spades. If you'd like to take in the first three but avoid the last, make this an early-morning walk.

Walk Facts

Start Ⓜ Széll Kálmán tér

End Ⓜ Clark Ádám tér

Length 1.2km; two hours

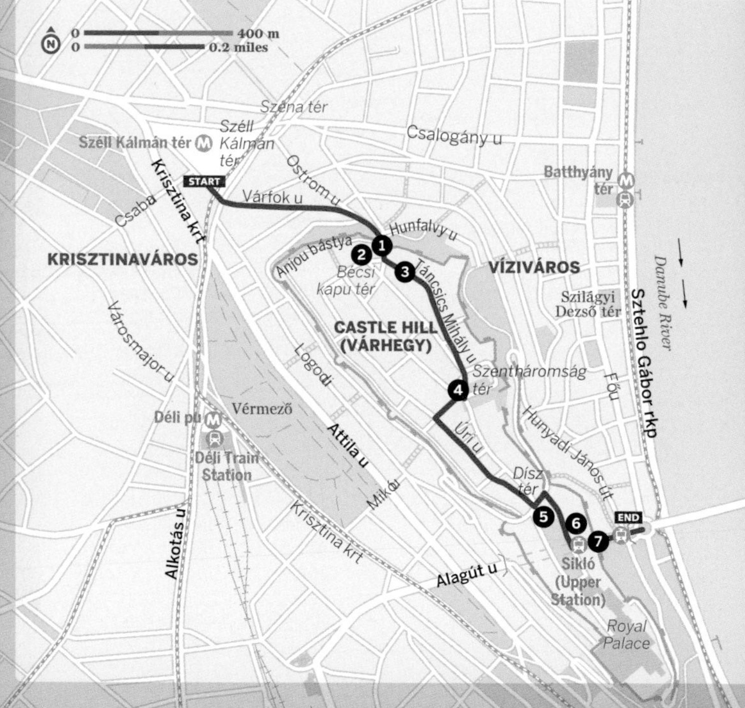

❶ Vienna Gate

Walk up Várfok utca from Széll Kálmán tér to **Vienna Gate** (Bécsi-kapu; 16, 16A, 116), the medieval entrance to the Old Town that was rebuilt in 1936 to mark the 250th anniversary of the castle being taken back from the Turks.

❷ National Archives

The large building to the west with the superbly coloured maiolica-tiled roof contains the **National Archives** (Országos Levéltár; 1920), which sometimes has exhibitions. To the west of Bécsi kapu tér (Vienna Gate Sq) – a weekend market in the Middle Ages – is an attractive group of four burgher houses at Nos 5 to 8.

❸ Táncsics Mihály Utca

Narrow **Táncsics Mihály utca** is full of little houses painted in lively hues and adorned with statues. In many courtyard entrances you'll see 13th-century stone niches called *sedilia* (perhaps used as merchant stalls). Further along the road to the southeast, at Táncsics Mihály utca 9, is the former prison where the leader of the 1848–49 War of Independence, Lajos Kossuth, was held from 1837 to 1840.

❹ Szentháromság Tér

The architecturally striking Hilton Budapest, incorporating parts of a medieval Dominican church and a baroque Jesuit college, is further south. In the centre of nearby **Szentháromság tér** is a replica of the Holy Trinity statue (Szentháromság szobor), a 'plague pillar' erected by grateful (and healthy) Buda citizens in the early 18th century.

❺ Former Ministry of Defence

Walking along Úri utca south to Dísz tér you'll come face to face with the bombed-out **former Ministry of Defence**, a casualty of WWII, and NATO's supposed nuclear target for Budapest during the Cold War. It's getting a long-overdue renovation and will eventually house the prime minister's office.

❻ Sándor Palace

Further south on the left is the restored **Sándor Palace** (Sándor-paklota; 1-224 5000; www.keh.hu; I Szent György tér 1-2; 16, 16A, 116), which now contains the offices of the president of the republic. A somewhat low-key (but ceremonial nonetheless) guard change takes place in front of the palace hourly between 9am and 6pm.

❼ Sikló

Just south of the upper station of the **Sikló** (www.bkv.hu; I Szent György tér & Clark Ádám tér; one way/return adult 1200/1800Ft, child 3-14yr 700/1100Ft; 7.30am-10pm, closed 1st & 3rd Mon of month; 16, 105, 19, 41) funicular are the Habsburg Steps, a 1903 ornamental gateway with steps leading down to the Royal Palace. Take the funicular down to Clark Ádám tér.

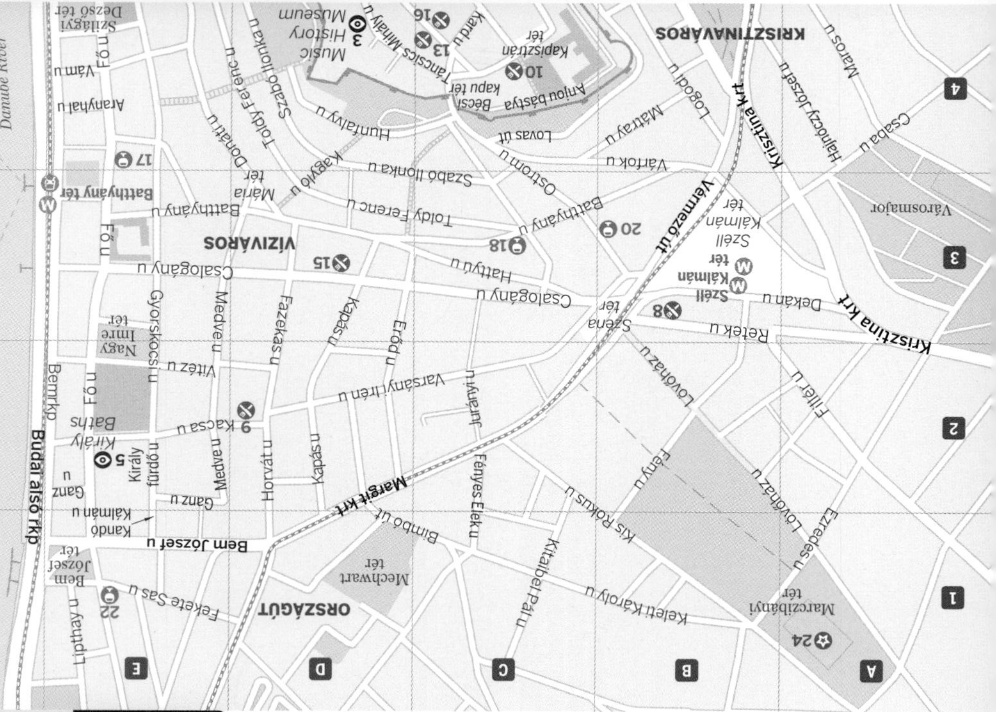

Danube River
Budai alsó rkp
Bemrkp
Lipthay u
Bem József tér
22
Fekete Sas u
Bem József u
Kandó Kálmán u
Ganz u
Király fürdő u
5 Király Baths
Fő u
Nagy Imre tér
Gyorskocsi u
Kacsa u
9
Medve u
Vitéz u
Horvát u
Fazekas u
Kapás u
Csalogány u
Vízíváros
15
Batthyány tér
17
Batthyány u
Mária tér
Donáti u
Toldy Ferenc u
Szabó Ilonka u
Kagyló u
Hunfalvy u
Music History Museum
3
Táncsics Mihály u
13
16
Kard u
Bécsi kapu tér
Anjou bástya
10
Kapisztrán tér
Lovas út
Ostrom u
Hattyú u
18
20
Aranyhal u
Vám u
Szilágyi Dezső tér
Országút
Mechwart tér
Bimbó út
Margit krt
Erőd u
Varsányi Irén u
Jurányi u
Fényes Elek u
Kitaibel Pál u
Kis Rókus u
Keleti Károly u
Fény u
Lövőház u
Széna tér
8
Széll Kálmán tér
Retek u
Dekán u
Fillér u
Ezredes u
Marczibányi tér
24
Vérmező út
Krisztina krt
Krisztinaváros
Várfok u
Mátray u
Logodi u
Hajnóczy József u
Csaba u
Maros u
Városmajor

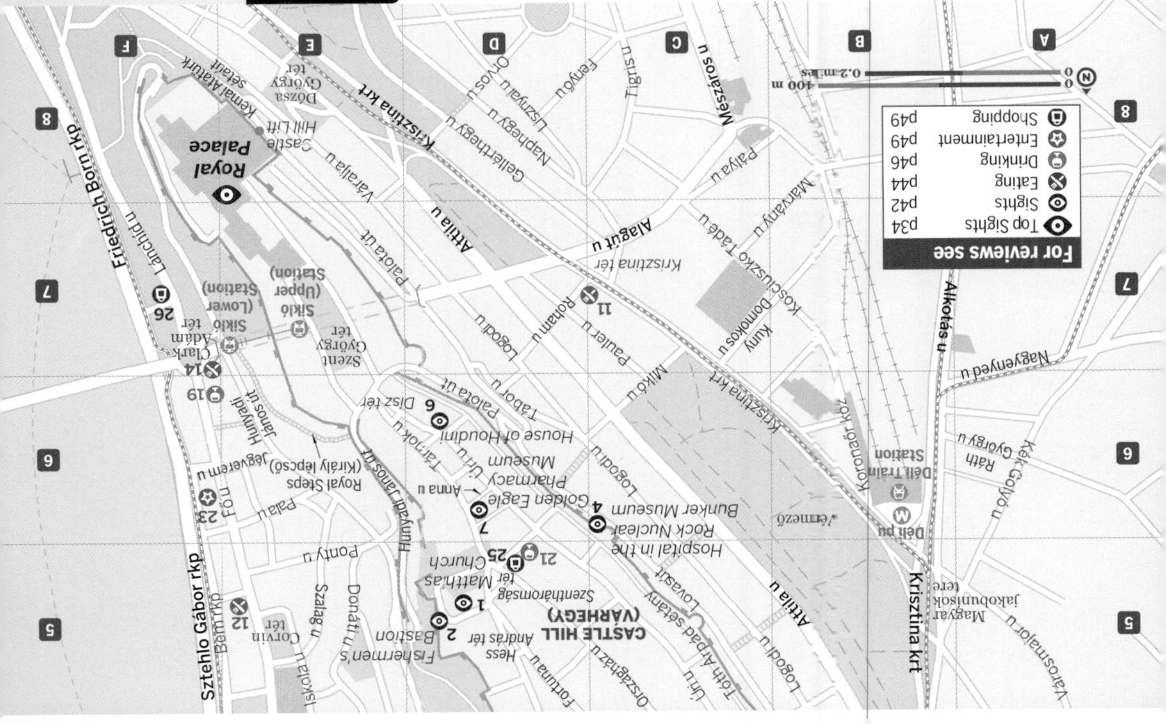

For reviews see

Top Sights	p34
Sights	p42
Eating	p44
Drinking	p46
Entertainment	p49
Shopping	p49

0 — 400 m
0 — 0.2 miles

A B C D E F
5 6 7 8

CASTLE HILL (VÁRHEGY)
Royal Palace
1 Matthias Church
2 Fishermen's Bastion
4 Hospital in the Rock Nuclear Bunker Museum
6 House of Houdini
7 Golden Eagle Pharmacy Museum
11
12
14
19
21
23
25
26
Sikló (Upper Station)
Sikló (Lower Station)
Castle Hill Lift
Royal Steps (Király lépcső)
Déli pu
Déli Train Station
Sztehlo Gábor rkp
Bem rkp
Friedrich Born rkp
Lánchíd u
Clark Ádám tér
Hunyadi János út
Jégverem u
Fő u
Pala u
Ponty u
Szalag u
Donáti u
Iskola u
Corvin tér
Hess András tér
Fortuna u
Országház u
Úri u
Tóth Árpád sétány
Lovas út
Szentháromság tér
Anna u
Tárnok u
Dísz tér
Szent György tér
Palota út
Tábor u
Logodi u
Attila u
Váralja u
Dózsa György tér
Kemal Atatürk sétaút
Krisztina krt
Gellérthegy u
Naphegy u
Lisznyai u
Orvos u
Fenyő u
Tigris u
Mészáros u
Pálya u
Márvány u
Alagút u
Krisztina tér
Roham u
Pauler u
Mikó u
Kosciuszko Tádé u
Kuny Domokos u
Koronaőr köz
Vérmező
Alkotás u
Nagyenyed u
Ráth György u
Kék Golyó u
Magyar jakobinusok tere
Városmajor u

Sights

Matthias Church CHURCH

1 MAP P40, D5

Parts of Matthias Church date back 500 years, notably the carvings above the southern entrance, but essentially the church (named after King Matthias Corvinus, who married Queen Beatrix here in 1474) is a neo-Gothic design by the architect Frigyes Schulek in 1896. The interior houses stained-glass windows, frescoes and wall decorations by the Romantic painters Károly Lotz and Bertalan Székely. (Mátyás templom; 1-489 0716; www.matyas-templom.hu; I Szentháromság tér 2; adult/concession 1500/1000Ft; 9am-5pm Mon-Fri, 9am-noon Sat, 1-5pm Sun; 16, 16A, 116)

Fishermen's Bastion MONUMENT

2 MAP P40, D5

The bastion, a neo-Gothic masquerade that looks medieval and offers some of the best views in Budapest, was built as a viewing platform in 1905 by Frigyes Schulek, the architect behind Matthias Church. Its name was taken from the medieval guild of fishermen responsible for defending this stretch of the castle wall. The seven white turrets represent the Magyar tribes that entered the Carpathian Basin in the late 9th century. (Halászbástya; I Szentháromság tér; adult/concession 1000/500Ft; 9am-8pm May–mid-Oct, to 7pm mid-Mar–Apr; 16, 16A, 116)

Music History Museum MUSEUM

3 MAP P40, D4

Housed in an 18th-century palace with a lovely courtyard, this wonderful little museum traces the development of music in Hungary from the 18th century to the present day in eight exhibition rooms. There are rooms devoted to the work of Béla Bartók, Franz Liszt, Zoltán Kodály and Joseph Haydn, with lots of instruments and original scores and manuscripts. Lovely place to spend an hour or two. (Zenetörténeti Múzeum; 1-214 6770; www.zti.hu/museum; I Táncsics Mihály utca 7; adult/6-26yr 600/300Ft; 10am-4pm Tue-Sun; 16, 16A, 116)

Hospital in the Rock Nuclear Bunker Museum MUSEUM

4 MAP P40, C6

Part of the Castle Hill caves network, this subterranean hospital was used extensively during the WWII siege of Budapest and during the 1956 Uprising. It contains original medical equipment as well as some 200 wax figures and is visited on a guided one-hour tour, which includes a walk through a Cold War–era nuclear bunker and an eight-minute introductory video. (Sziklakórház Atombunker Múzeum; 06 70 701 0101; www.sziklakorhaz.eu; I Lovas út 4/c; adult/concession 4000/2000Ft; 10am-8pm; 5, 16)

Király Baths

BATHHOUSE

5 MAP P40, E2

The four pools for soaking here, with water temperatures of between 26°C and 40°C, are genuine Turkish baths erected in 1570. The largest has a wonderful skylit central dome (though the place is begging for a renovation); the other three, including the immersion pool, are small. The Király is open to both men and women daily so bring a swimsuit. (Király Gyógyfürdő; 1-202 3688; www.kiralyfurdo.hu; II Fő utca 84; daily ticket incl locker/cabin adult 2500/2800Ft, student 1900/2200Ft, senior 1500/1800Ft; 9am-9pm; 109, 4, 6, 19, 41)

House of Houdini

MUSEUM

6 MAP P40, D6

Dedicated to the famous Hungarian-born magician and escape artist Harry Houdini, who was born Erik Weisz in Budapest's district VII in 1874, this small museum offers a cabinet of curiosities featuring original items from Houdini's life, such as personal letters, handcuffs and documents, as well as props from the US *Houdini* miniseries (2014). At the end of the guided tour, guests are treated to a live 15-minute magic performance. A gem of a small museum and loads of fun. (1-951 8066; www.houseofhoudinibudapest.com; I Dísz tér 11; €6.50; 10am-7pm; 16, 16A, 116)

Fishermen's Bastion

BRIAN KINNEY / SHUTTERSTOCK ©

Going Up & Down

A real 'insider's' way to get to and from Castle Hill is from I Dózsa tér (take bus 16 from Pest), where you'll find a **lift** (Map p40, E8; 200Ft; 6am-8.30pm Mon-Sat, 9am-6.30pm Sun; 16, 16A) that will whisk you up to the Lion Court and National Széchenyi Library located in the heart of Castle Hill. Glass cases in the hallway where the lift starts and ends are filled with archaeological artefacts found in the Royal Palace.

Golden Eagle Pharmacy Museum

MUSEUM

7 MAP P40, D6

Just north of Dísz tér, on the site of Budapest's first pharmacy (1681), this small, entertaining museum contains a mock-up of an alchemist's laboratory, with dried bats and stuffed crocodiles suspended from the ceiling, a small 'spice rack' used by 17th-century travellers for their daily fixes of curative herbs, curiously shaped glassware and a blackened mummy head. (Arany Sas Patikamúzeum; 1-375 9772; www.semmelweis.museum.hu; I Tárnok utca 18; adult/concession 800/400Ft; 10am-6pm Tue-Sun Mar-Oct, 10am-4pm Tue-Fri, 10am-6pm Sat & Sun Nov-Mar; 16, 16A, 116)

Eating

À Table

BAKERY €

8 MAP P40, B3

Branch of a popular bakery chain that has charmed Budapest with excellent pastries, Danishes and savoury snacks, such as quiche. (www.atable.hu; II Retek utca 6; cakes 490-790Ft; 7am-7pm Mon-Fri, 7am-6pm Sat, 8am-6pm Sun; M M2 Széll Kálmán tér, 4, 6)

Mandragóra

HUNGARIAN €€

9 MAP P40, D2

With a hint of black magic in its name and a cosy location in the basement of a residential block, this family-run restaurant has earned loyal local fans with its excellent takes on Hungarian classics. Feast on slow-cooked duck with beetroot, grey-cattle sausage or pearl-barley risotto. The two-/three-course lunches are a bargain at 2500/2850Ft. (06 20 532 8993, 1-202 2165; www.mandragorakavehaz.hu; II Kacsa utca 22; mains 3000-5600Ft; 11am-11pm Mon-Sat; 11, 4, 6)

Baltazár Grill & Wine Bar

STEAK €€

10 MAP P40, C4

Free-range chicken, sea bass, juicy rib-eyes and burgers sizzle on the charcoal grill at this excellent restaurant. Classic Hungarian dishes are also well represented, with several vegetarian dishes completing the picture. If you're not feeling peckish, you might make your way to the atmospheric Baltazár wine bar instead to sample some tipples from all over Central Europe. (1-300 7050; www.baltazarbudapest.com; I Országház utca 3; mains 3360-9680Ft; noon-11pm; 16, 16A, 116)

Bistro Déryné BISTRO €€

11 MAP P40, C7

What used to be a traditional cafe near the entrance to the Alagút (the tunnel under Castle Hill), established the year WWI broke out, is now a stylish bistro with excellent breakfasts and more substantial meals (duck confit, wild boar *paprikás,* slow-braised beef brisket) throughout the day. Great horseshoe-shaped bar plus music, a lovely terrace, an open kitchen and always a warm welcome. (1-225 1407; www.bistroderyne.com; I Krisztina tér 3; mains 3650-4280Ft; 7.30am-midnight Mon-Thu, to 1am Fri, 9am-1am Sat, to midnight Sun; 5, 178, 56, 56A)

Horgásztanya Vendéglő SEAFOOD €€

12 MAP P40, E5

A classic restaurant by the Danube where freshwater-fish soup (from 1550Ft) is served in bowls, pots or kettles, and your carp, catfish or trout might be prepared Baja , Tisza- or more spicy Szeged-style. A must-try. (Fisherfarm Restaurant; 1-212 3780; www.horgasztanyavendeglo.hu; II Fő utca 27; mains 1550-3800Ft; noon-midnight; ; 19, 41)

21 Magyar Vendéglő HUNGARIAN €€

13 MAP P40, C4

It may have the less-than-inspiring name '21 Hungarian Restaurant' but this place serves up some wonderfully innovative modern takes on traditional Hungarian dishes such as veal *pörkölt* (a kind of stew like goulash) and chicken *paprikás* (a variation of *pörkölt* with sour cream). There is super old/new decor as well as friendly service, and it even bottles its very own wine. (1-202 2113; www.21restaurant.hu; I Fortuna utca 21; mains 3489-4980Ft; noon-midnight; 16, 16A, 116)

Leo Budapest INTERNATIONAL €€€

14 MAP P40, F7

There are rooftop bar-restaurants and then there's His Highness Leo on the 8th floor of the Hotel Clark, with views of the Royal Palace above and the Danube below. Food (burgers, gyros, sausages, steak) is pricey but OK; try one of the sublime cocktails (from 2850Ft). Bookings are essential. (06 70 882 7777; www.leo-budapest.hu; I Clark Ádám tér 1, Hotel Clark; mains 4900-13,800Ft; noon-midnight; 16, 105, 19, 41)

Csalogány 26 INTERNATIONAL €€€

15 MAP P40, D3

The decor is spartan at this intimate restaurant, which turns its creativity to preparing its superb food. Try the roasted lamb served with butter squash *lecsó* (a kind of ratatouille, 5000Ft) or other meat-heavy dishes that make the most of the wonderful local ingredients. An eight-course tasting menu costs 6000Ft (23,000Ft with matching wines) though there is also a budget-pleasing three-course set lunch that is on offer on weekdays, costing just 3100Ft. (1-201 7892; www.csalogany26.hu; I Csalogány utca 26; mains 4500-6500Ft; noon-3pm & 7-10pm Tue-Sat; 11, 39, 111)

Pierrot INTERNATIONAL €€€

16 MAP P40, C4

This stylish, long-established restaurant, which is housed in what was a bakery in the Middle Ages, specialises in serving up dishes of the Austro-Hungarian Empire, revamped for the 21st century. Expect to sample the likes of pike-perch and prawn *paprikás*, duck leg wrapped in pastry with apple cabbage, and confit piglet cheek. Presentation of the dishes is faultless; eat in the vaulted dining room, the covered side court or garden. (1-375 6971; www.pierrot.hu; I Fortuna utca 14; mains 3780-8910Ft; noon-midnight; 16, 16A, 116)

Drinking

Steamhouse Cafe CAFE

17 MAP P40, E4

This lovely new cafe on the top floor of the one-time Batthyány tér covered market takes its coffee very seriously indeed, with blends from Colombia to Ethiopia. But we come here for the food too, with breakfast (890Ft to 2950Ft) available all day every day and the daily one-plate lunch a steal at just 1290Ft. Super views across the Danube are free. (06 70 349 0259; www.facebook.com/steamhousebudapest; I Batthyány tér 5-6; 8am-7pm Mon-Fri, 9am-3pm; M M2 Batthyány tér)

Bereg Bar & Cafe CAFE

18 MAP P40, C3

Located in Swan House, a remarkable example of Hungarian 'organic architecture', this friendly place welcomes 'wanderers, lovers, artists' and more. There's a peaceful garden for lingering over a craft beer, a glass of Hungarian wine or a coffee. Light meals (dishes 1390Ft to 2290Ft) available. Friendly service too. (1-615 1298; http://beregbar.hu; II Batthyány utca 49; 8am-11pm Mon-Fri, noon-11pm Sat & Sun; 16, 16A, 116)

Lánchíd Söröző BAR

As its name implies, this pub – now in its 29th year – is situated right at the Chain Bridge head and has a wonderful retro Magyar feel to it, with old movie posters and advertisements adorning the walls and red-checked cloths on the tables. This is a proper local place with friendly service. Food is available (dishes cost from 1850Ft to 2650Ft) too. (Chain Bridge Pub; 1-214 3144; www.lanchidsorozo.hu; I Fő utca 4; 10am-midnight; 16, 16A, 86, 19, 41)

Oscar American Bar BAR

20 MAP P40, B3

The decor is cinema-inspired (Hollywood memorabilia on the wood-panelled walls, leather directors' chairs) and the beautiful crowd often act like they're on camera. Not to worry: the potent cocktails (950Ft to 2250Ft) – from daiquiris and cosmopolitans to champagne cocktails and mojitos – go down a treat. There's music most nights. (06 70 700 0222; http://oscarbar budapest.hu; I Ostrom utca 14; 5pm-midnight Wed, to 4am Thu-Sat; M M2 Széll Kálmán tér)

Ruszwurm Cukrászda CAFE

21 MAP P40, D5

This diminutive cafe dating from 1827 is the perfect place for coffee and cakes (550Ft to 750Ft) in the Castle District. Be warned: in high season it's almost always impossible to get a seat – inside or out. (1-375 5284; www.ruszwurm.hu; I Szentháromság utca 7; 10am-7pm Mon-Fri, to 6pm Sat & Sun; 16, 16A, 116)

Pierrot

Bambi Eszpresszó

CAFE

22 MAP P40, E1

Named after a communist-era local soft drink, Bambi Eszpresszó has hardly changed since the 1960s and that's just the way the clientele here likes it. Friendly though set-it-down-with-a-crash service is part of the picture. (1-212 3171; www.facebook.com/bambieszpresszo; II Frankel Leó utca 2-4; 7am-10pm Mon-Fri, 9am-10pm Sat & Sun; 19, 41)

The Wines of Hungary

Wine has been made in Hungary since at least the time of the Romans. It is very much a part of Hungarian culture, but only in recent years has it moved on from the local tipple you drank at Sunday lunch or the overwrought and overpriced thimble of rarefied red sipped in a Budapest wine bar to the all-singin', all-dancin', all-embracin' obsession that it is today.

Wine Regions

Hungary is divided into seven major wine-growing regions, but we're most interested in a half-dozen of their subdivisions. It's all a matter of taste but the most distinctive and exciting Hungarian red wines come from Eger in the Northern Uplands and Villány in Southern Transdanubia. The best dry whites are produced around Lake Balaton's northern shore and in Somló, though the latest craze is for bone-dry *furmint* from Tokaj, which also makes the world-renowned sweet wine.

Choosing & Buying Wine

Wine is sold by the glass or bottle everywhere and usually at reasonable prices. Old-fashioned wine bars ladle out plonk by the *deci* (decilitre, or 0.1L), but if you're into more serious wine, you should visit one of Budapest's excellent wine bars, such as **DiVino Borbár** (p99), **Doblo** (p125) or **Palack Borbár** (p62). Among speciality wine shops are those in the **Bortársaság** (p49) chain and the **Malatinszky Wine Store** (p101).

When choosing a Hungarian wine, look for the words *minőségi bor* (quality wine) or *különleges minőségi bor* (premium quality wine). On a wine label the first word indicates the region, the second the grape variety (eg Villányi *kékfrankos*) or the type or brand of wine (eg Tokaji Aszú, Szekszárdi Bikavér). Other important words that you'll see include *édes* (sweet), *fehér* (white), *félédes* (semisweet), *félszáraz* (semidry or medium), *pezsgő* (sparkling), *száraz* (dry) and *vörös* (red).

Entertainment

Budavár Cultural Centre

LIVE MUSIC

23 MAP P40, F6

This cultural centre just below Buda Castle has frequent programs for children and adults, including the excellent Sebő Klub és Táncház at 7pm on the first or second Saturday of every month and the Regejáró Misztrál Folk Music Club at the same time on the last Sunday. (Budavári Művelődési Háza; 1-201 0324, box office 1-201 7158; www.bem6.hu; I Bem rakpart 6; programs 800-2000Ft; box office 9am-3pm Mon-Wed, 1-7pm Fri; 19, 41)

Marczibányi tér Cultural Centre

LIVE MUSIC

24 MAP P40, A1

This venue has Hungarian, Moldavian, Slovakian and Csángó dance and music by Guzsalyas (adult/student 1200/800Ft) usually on Thursdays, starting at 7pm. (Marczibányi téri Művelődési Központ; 1-212 2820; www.marczi.hu; II Marczibányi tér 5/a; performances 800-5000Ft; 149, 4, 6)

Shopping

Herend

CERAMICS

25 MAP P40, D5

For both contemporary and traditional fine porcelain, there is no other place to go but Herend, Hungary's answer to Wedgwood. Among the most popular motifs produced by the company is the Victoria pattern of butterflies and wildflowers, designed for the British queen during the mid-19th century. (06 20 241 3880, 1-225 1051; www.herend.com; I Szentháromság utca 5; 10am-6pm Mon-Fri, to 4pm Sat & Sun Apr-Oct, 10am-6pm Mon-Fri, to 2pm Sat Nov-Mar; 16, 16A, 116)

Bortársaság

WINE

26 MAP P40, F7

Once known as the Budapest Wine Society, this place has a dozen or so retail outlets in the capital with an exceptional selection of Hungarian wines. No one, but no one, knows Hungarian wines like these guys do. Now in a more central Buda location. (06 20 518 0780; www.bortarsasag.hu; I Lánchíd utca 5; 10am-9pm Mon-Fri, to 7pm Sat; M M2 Széll Kálmán tér, 4, 6)

Explore Gellért Hill & Tabán

Standing atop Gellért Hill, the lovely Liberty Monument looks down on the Tabán, a leafy, once very Serbian neighbourhood dating to the 17th century. Today the greater area is home to the prestigious Budapest University of Technology and Economics (BME) and its students. The main thoroughfare, Bartók Béla út, is fast laying claim to being the 'happening' part of south Buda.

The Short List

- ***Liberty Monument (p55)*** *Taking in the incomparable views of Castle Hill, the Danube and Pest from the top of Gellért Hill.*
- ***Gellért Baths (p52)*** *Soaking in this opulent art nouveau thermal spa, an experience described as having a bath in a cathedral.*
- ***Castle Garden Bazaar (p58)*** *Reaching Castle Hill by walking through this recently renovated pleasure garden.*

Getting There & Around

Bus 7 to XI Szent Gellért tér from V Ferenciek tere in Pest. Bus 27 runs to Gellért Hill from XI Móricz Zsigmond körtér.

M The M4 metro line for XI Gellért tér and XI Móricz Zsigmond körtér.

Tram 18 from Déli station and 19 from I Batthyány tér to XI Szent Gellért tér. Trams 47 and 49 from XI Szent Gellért tér to Pest and the Little Ring Road.

Gellért Hill & Tabán Map on p56

Liberty Monument (p55) looking over Budapest

Top Sight

Gellért Baths

Soaking in the thermal waters of the art nouveau Gellért Baths, open to both men and women in mixed areas, is an awesome experience. The six thermal pools range in temperature from 35°C to 40°C, and the water – high in calcium, magnesium and hydrogen carbonate – is said to be good for joint pains, arthritis, blood circulation and asthma.

MAP P56, D4

Gellért Gyógyfürdő

06 30 849 9514

www.gellertbath.hu

XI Kelenhegyi út 4, Danubius Hotel Gellért

6am-8pm

7, 86, M4 Szent Gellért tér, 18, 19, 47, 49

History

The springs here were favoured by the Turks as they were hotter than the others in Buda. In the 17th century the site was named Sárosfürdő (Mud Bath) after the fine silt that was pushed up with the spring water and settled at the bottom of the pools. The Gellért Baths as we know them today opened in 1918; they were expanded in 1927 with an outdoor wave bath and in 1934 with an indoor effervescent whirlpool.

Visiting the Baths

At the Gellért Baths (like most other baths nowadays) you are given an electronic bracelet that directs you to and then opens your locker or cabin. In the past it was a bit more complicated: you would find a free locker or cabin yourself and – after you got changed in (or beside) it – you would call the attendant, who would lock it for you and hand you a numbered tag. You had to remember your locker number; in a bid to prevent thefts, the number on the tag was not the same as the one on the locker.

Swimming Pools

The swimming pools (included in the price) at the Gellért are mixed. The indoor ones, open year-round, are the most beautiful in Budapest; the outdoor wave pool (open May to September) has lovely landscaped gardens and 26°C water. The thermal one is 36°C.

★ Top Tips

- Along with a bathing suit (which can be rented for 2000Ft if needed), you might want to bring a pair of flip-flops (thongs), and a towel, as the sheets provided are not very absorbent.
- Everyone must use a bathing cap in the swimming pools; bring your own or use the disposable ones for 1000Ft.

✕ Take a Break

On trendifying XI Bartók Béla út, just around the corner from the baths, you'll find several eating options.

Vegan Love (p59) serves oh-so-healthy and rather unusual vegan street food.

Kelet Cafe & Gallery (p61), filled with used books and newspapers, serves soups and salads along with the usual coffee and cakes.

Top Sight

Citadella & Liberty Monument

The Citadella atop Gellért Hill is a fortress that never saw battle. Built by the Habsburgs after the 1848–49 War of Independence to defend against further insurrection, by the time it was ready five years later the political climate had changed. To the southeast stands the Liberty Monument, the lovely lady with a palm frond in her outstretched arms proclaiming freedom.

MAP P56, C3

Citadel

27

Citadella

The Citadella is an oblong structure measuring 220m by 60m and built around a courtyard. It was given to the city in the 1890s, and parts of it were symbolically blown to pieces. Today the fortress contains some big guns peeping through its loopholes, but the interior has been closed to the public while its future is decided.

Liberty Monument

Standing 14m high, the monument was erected in 1947 to honour the Soviet soldiers who died liberating Budapest in 1945. But the names of the fallen and the statues of the soldiers themselves were removed in 1992, and sent to what is now called Memento Park (p64).

Cave Church

On the way up the Gellért Hill, have a peek at the **Cave Church** (Sziklatemplom; www.sziklatemplom.hu; XI Szent Gellért rakpart 1/a; adult/child 600/500Ft; ⏲9.30am-7.30pm Mon-Sat; Ⓜ M4 Szent Gellért tér, 🚋41, 47, 49, 18, 19), built into a cave in 1926 and the seat of the Pauline order here until 1951, when the priests were imprisoned by the communists and the cave sealed off. It was reopened and reconsecrated in 1992.

Liberty & Elizabeth Bridges

The spans across the Danube below are (to the south) **Liberty Bridge** (Szabadság-híd; Ⓜ M4 Szent Gellért tér, 🚋47, 49) and (to the north) **Elizabeth Bridge** (Erzsébet-híd; 🚌7, 86, 🚋19). The former, which opened in time for the Millenary Exhibition in 1896, has a *fin-de-siècle* cantilevered span and was rebuilt in the same style immediately after WWII. Gleaming white Elizabeth Bridge, dating from 1964, enjoys a special place in the hearts of many Budapesters as it was the first newly designed bridge to reopen after WWII, when the retreating and vengeful Germans had destroyed all the bridges.

★ Top Tips

- From the Citadella walk northwest for a few minutes along Citadella sétány to a lookout with one of the best vantage points in Budapest.
- To get to the Citadella on foot from the Cave Church, follow XI Verejték utca (Perspiration St) through the trees.
- To avoid the steep climb, hop on bus 27.

✕ Take a Break

For a proper sit-down meal, walk down the steps behind the St Gellért Monument and head north to Aranyszarvas (p59). It serves some excellent (and unusual) game dishes.

You could also walk down to Bartók Béla út to Marcello (p59), which has been dispensing excellent pizza and other Italian dishes to students in the area for over two decades.

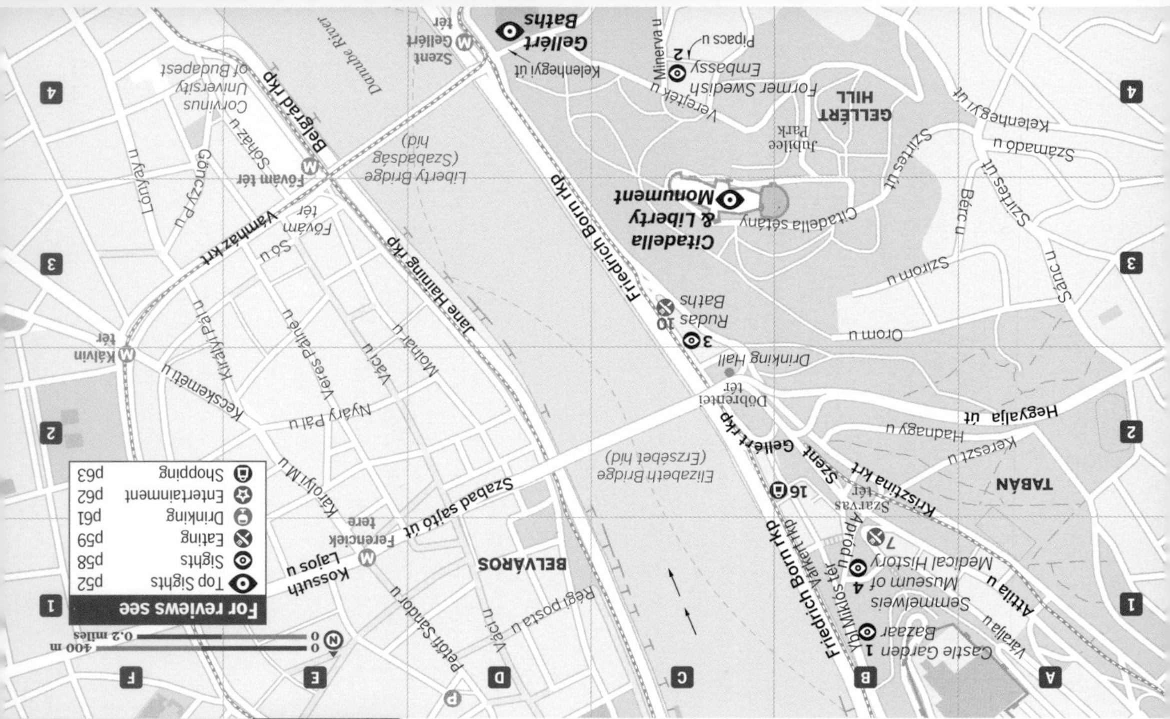

For reviews see

Top Sights	p52
Sights	p58
Eating	p59
Drinking	p61
Entertainment	p62
Shopping	p63

0 400 m
0 0.2 miles

A B C D E F
1 2 3 4

Castle Garden Bazaar 1
Semmelweis Museum of Medical History 4
7
16
3
Rudas Baths 10
Drinking Hall
Citadella & Liberty Monument
Former Swedish Embassy 2
Gellért Baths
Jubilee Park
GELLÉRT HILL
TABÁN
BELVÁROS
Danube River
Elizabeth Bridge (Erzsébet híd)
Liberty Bridge (Szabadság híd)
Corvinus University of Budapest
Friedrich Born rkp
Jane Haining rkp
Belgrád rkp
Várkert rkp
Ybl Miklós tér
Apród u
Szarvas tér
Krisztina krt
Szent Gellért rkp
Döbrentei tér
Attila u
Váralja u
Hegyalja út
Hadnagy u
Kereszt u
Orom u
Szirom u
Sánc u
Bérc u
Szirtes út
Számadó u
Kelenhegyi út
Citadella sétány
Verejték u
Minerva u
Pipacs u
Szent Gellért tér
Szabad sajtó út
Kossuth Lajos u
Ferenciek tere
Petőfi Sándor u
Régi posta u
Váci u
Károlyi M u
Nyáry Pál u
Veres Pálné u
Molnár u
Kecskeméti u
Királyi Pál u
Kálvin tér
Só u
Fővám tér
Vámház krt
Gönczy P u
Lónyay u
Sóház u

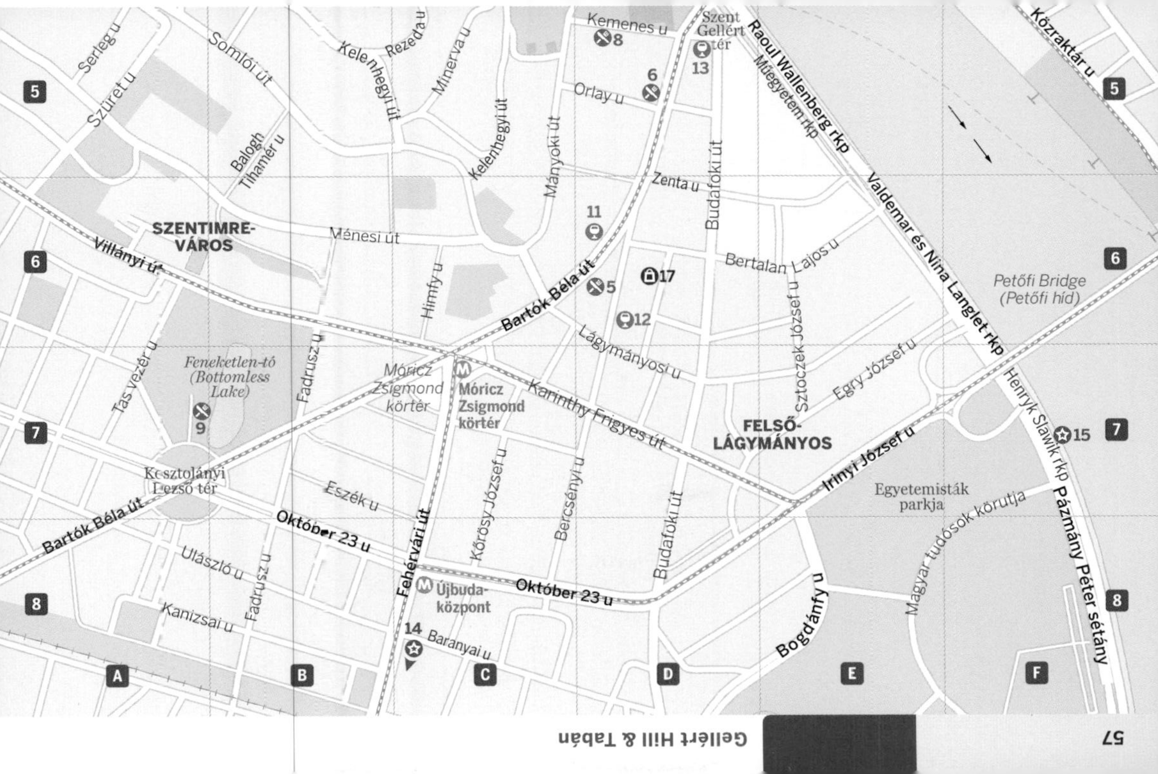
Kemenes u
Szent Gellért tér
Közraktár u
Serleg u
Somlói út
Kelenhegyi út
Rezeda u
Minerva u
8
6
13
Orlay u
Raoul Wallenberg rkp
Műegyetem rkp
Szüret u
Balogh Tihamér u
Kelenhegyi út
Mányoki út
Budafoki út
Zenta u
11
SZENTIMRE-VÁROS
Ménesi út
Villányi út
Valdemar és Nina Langlet rkp
Bartók Béla út
17
5
Bertalan Lajos u
Himfy u
Petőfi Bridge (Petőfi híd)
12
Sztoczek József u
Lágymányosi u
Fadrusz u
Feneketlen-tó (Bottomless Lake)
Móricz Zsigmond körtér
Egry József u
Tas vezér u
Karinthy Frigyes út
9
FELSŐ-LÁGYMÁNYOS
Henryk Slawik rkp
15
Irinyi József u
Kosztolányi Dezső tér
Kőrösy József u
Bercsényi u
Eszék u
Egyetemisták parkja
Magyar tudósok körútja
Budafoki út
Október 23 u
Pázmány Péter sétány
Uászló u
Fehérvári út
Újbuda-központ
Bogdánfy u
Kanizsai u
14
Baranyai u
A
B
C
D
E
F
5
6
7
8

Sights

Castle Garden Bazaar
HISTORIC SITE

1 MAP P56, B1

This renovated pleasure park dating from 1893 has added a whole new dimension to Tabán district in recent years. The complex comprises over a dozen neo-Gothic and neo-Renaissance structures, including a theatre, convention centre and, in both the **Southern Palaces** and the **Guard's Palace**, large galleries with cutting-edge exhibitions. A staircase and lift from Lánchíd utca lead to the **Neo-Renaissance Garden**. To get up to **Castle Hill** (Várhegy; 16, 16A, 116, M M2 Batthyány tér, Széll Kálmán tér, 19, 41), there are stairs, lifts and an escalator. (Várkert Bazár; 1-225 0554; www.varkertbazar.hu; Ybl Miklós tér 6; exhibitions adult 2000-3000Ft, concession 1000-1500Ft; 10am-6pm Tue-Sun; 86, 19, 41)

Former Swedish Embassy
NOTABLE BUILDING

2 MAP P56, C4

The former Swedish Embassy on Gellért Hill bears a plaque attesting to the heroism of Raoul Wallenberg, a Swedish diplomat and businessman who, along with others including Carl-Ivan Danielsson and Per Anger, rescued as many as 35,000 Hungarian Jews during WWII. (XI Minerva utca 3a/b; 27)

Rudas Baths
BATHHOUSE

3 MAP P56, C3

Built in 1566, these renovated baths are the most Turkish in Budapest, with an octagonal main pool, domed cupola with coloured glass and massive columns. It's a real zoo on mixed weekend nights, when bathing costumes (rental 1500Ft) are compulsory. (Rudas Gyógyfürdő; 1-356 1322; http://en.rudasfurdo.hu; I Döbrentei tér 9; incl cabin Mon-Fri/Sat & Sun 3500/4000Ft, morning/night ticket 2800/5100Ft; men 6am-8pm Mon & Wed-Fri, women 6am-8pm Tue, mixed 10pm-4am Fri, 6am-8pm & 10pm-4am Sat, 6am-8pm Sun; 7, 86, 18, 19)

Semmelweis Museum of Medical History
MUSEUM

4 MAP P56, B1

This quirky museum traces the history of medicine from Graeco-Roman times through medical tools and photographs. Much is made about the life and works of Ignác Semmelweis (1818–65), the 'saviour of mothers', who discovered the cause of puerperal (childbirth) fever but whose observations were not accepted in his life. Dr Semmelweis was born in this house. (Semmelweis Orvostörténeti Múzeum; 1-375 3533, 1-201 1577; www.semmelweis.museum.hu; I Apród utca 1-3; adult/child 1000/500Ft; 10am-6pm Tue-Sun Mar-Oct, 10am-4pm Tue-Fri, to 6pm Sat & Sun Nov-Feb; 86, 19, 41)

Eating

Marcello

ITALIAN €

5 MAP P56, D6

Longtime favourite with students from the nearby university since it opened almost three decades ago, this family-owned operation located just down the road from XI Szent Gellért tér offers reliable Italian fare at affordable prices. The pizzas (1350Ft to 1900Ft) and the salad bar are good value, as is the lasagne (1800Ft), which is legendary in these parts. (06 30 243 5229, 1-466 6231; www.marcelloetterem.hu/en; XI Bartók Béla út 40; mains 1600-3600Ft; noon-10pm Sun-Wed, to 11pm Thu-Sat; 19, 47, 49)

Vegan Love

VEGAN €

6 MAP P56, D5

Vegan fast (sorry, street) food doesn't get much better than at this hole-in-the-wall eatery on up-and-coming XI Bartók Béla út. Try the likes of sweet potato or curry lentil burgers, the vegan chilli tofu hot dog or Philly cheese steak sandwich. Small/large servings from the salad bar cost 700/1400Ft. (www.veganlove.hu; XI Bartók Béla út 9; mains 1100-2000Ft; 11am-9pm; ; M M4 Móricz Zsigmond körtér, 18, 19, 47, 49)

Aranyszarvas

HUNGARIAN €€

7 MAP P56, B1

Set in an 18th-century inn literally down the steps from the southern end of Castle Hill (views!), the

Castle Garden Bazaar

'Golden Stag' serves up some very meaty and unusual dishes (try the venison that is served in fruity game sauce with dumplings, wild-boar stew or the duck breast dressed with orange sauce). The covered outside terrace is a delightful place to sit in the warmer months. (☎06 30 476 2950; http://aranyszarvasetterem.hu/en; I Szarvas tér 1; mains 3500-4500Ft; ⊙noon-10pm; 🚌5, 86, 🚋18, 19, 41)

Pagony Kert GASTROPUB **€€**

8 MAP P56, D5

Set up in and around the disused pools that were once part of the neighbouring Gellért Baths

Raoul Wallenberg, Hero for All Times

Raoul Wallenberg (1912–47) began working in 1936 for a trading firm whose owner was a Hungarian Jew. In July 1944 the Swedish Foreign Ministry, at the request of Jewish and refugee organisations in the USA, sent the 32-year-old Swede ostensibly as an attaché on a rescue mission to Budapest to their embassy there. By that time almost half a million Jews in Hungary had been sent to Nazi death camps in Germany and Poland.

Wallenberg immediately began issuing Swedish safe-conduct passes (nicknamed 'Wallenberg passports') from the Swedish embassy in Budapest. He also set up a series of 'safe houses' (mostly in Újlipótváros and now marked with pavement plaques) flying the flag of Sweden and other neutral countries where Jews could seek asylum. He even followed German 'death marches' and deportation trains, distributing food and clothing, and actually pulling some 500 people off the cars along the way.

When the Soviet army entered Budapest in January 1945, Wallenberg went to report to the authorities but in the wartime confusion was arrested for espionage and sent to Moscow. In the early 1950s, responding to reports that Wallenberg had been seen alive in a labour camp, the Soviet Union announced that he had in fact died of a heart attack two years after the war ended. Many believe Wallenberg was executed by the Soviets, who suspected him of spying for the USA.

Wallenberg was made an honorary citizen of Budapest in 2003. Other foreigners associated with helping Hungarian Jews in Budapest include Carl Lutz (1885–1975), a Swiss consul who has a memorial devoted to him on VII Dob utca in Pest, and Jane Haining (1897–1944), a Budapest-based Scottish missionary who died in Auschwitz. In 2010 the city of Budapest named sections of the Danube riverbanks in honour of these courageous people.

complex, Pagony Kert is an unusual warm-weather venue. Located entirely outdoors, this seasonal self-service eatery on the slopes of Gellért Hill is a unique place to enjoy a glass of wine, a tasty burger or a salad. (06 31 783 6411; www.pagonykert.hu; Kemenes utca 10; mains 2290-3590Ft; 9am-10pm Mon-Fri, from 11am Sat & Sun; 7, M4 Szent Gellért tér, 19, 47, 49)

Hemingway INTERNATIONAL €€

9 MAP P56, A7

This very stylish eatery, located in a fabulous location in a small park overlooking legendary Feneketlen-tó (Bottomless Lake) in south Buda, has a varied and ever-changing menu as well as a wonderfully spacious terrace. There are lots of vegetarian dishes on offer (2680Ft to 3480Ft) should you want something light and easy to eat, and Sunday brunch (4900Ft; with unlimited drinks 6200Ft) is a perennial crowd-pleaser. (1-381 0522, 06 30 488 6000; http://hemingway-etterem.hu; XI Kosztolányi Dezső tér 2; mains 3590-6250Ft; noon-midnight Mon-Sat, to 4pm Sun; 7, M4 Móricz Zsigmond körtér, 19, 49)

Rudas Bistro INTERNATIONAL €€€

10 MAP P56, C3

We love, love, love this place with its turquoise interior and stunning views of the Danube and bridges. It sits above the Rudas Baths Wellness Centre (ask about inclusive packages) so it's just the ticket after a relaxing massage or treatment. The smallish outside terrace is a delight in summer (though it can be noisy). (06 20 538 2903; www.rudasrestaurant.hu; Döbrentei tér 9, Rudas Baths; mains 3790-6890Ft; 11am-10pm; 7, 86, 18, 19)

Drinking

Kelet Cafe & Gallery CAFE

11 MAP P56, D6

This super-cool cafe moonlights as a used-book exchange on the ground floor and boasts a large, bright gallery with additional seating upstairs. There are foreign newspapers to read, and soups (890Ft to 1100Ft), sandwiches (from 1200Ft) and fried rice or curry (1890Ft) should you feel peckish. Try the super hot chocolate. (Kelet Kávézó és Galéria; 06 20 456 5507; www.facebook.com/keletkavezo; XI Bartók Béla út 29; 7.30am-11pm Mon-Fri, 9am-11pm Sat & Sun; M4 Móricz Zsigmond körtér, 18, 19, 47, 49)

B8 Pub CRAFT BEER

12 MAP P56, D6

A favourite new watering hole in Buda, this pint-sized pub (though there are three tiny floors) has some 55 craft beers available from Hungary's five dozen breweries. Look for the names Legenda, Monyo and Etyeki, and try the

Drinking Cure

If you don't like getting wet or you don't have the time for a thermal bath, do what locals do and try a 'drinking cure' by visiting the **Drinking Hall** (Ivócsarnok; Map p56, C2; 11am-6pm Mon, Wed & Fri, 7am-2pm Tue & Thu), a hot and humid room just below the western end of Elizabeth Bridge. A half-litre/litre of the hot, smelly water, which is meant to cure whatever ails you, is a steal at just 30/60Ft. Bring your own container.

last's Belga Búza (Belgian Wheat) beer. Harder stuff? Some 10 types of *pálinka* (fruit brandy) are available. (B8 Kézműves Sör és Pálinkabár; 1-791 3462; www.facebook.com/b8pub; XI Bercsenyi utca 8; 4-11pm; M M4 Móricz Zsigmind körtér, 18, 19, 47, 49)

Palack Borbár

WINE BAR

13 MAP P56, D5

We are pleased to see a real wine bar open on the Buda side, with well over 100 types from a dozen Hungarian regions available by the 1.5dL (150mL) glass (650Ft to 2200Ft), with accompanying sliced meats and cheese plates (1690Ft to 2690Ft) that traditionally act as blotter here. Tapas (650Ft to 1490Ft) available. Great place to buy a bottle too. (Bottle Wine Bar; 06 30 997 1902; http://palackborbar.hu; Szent Gellért tér 3; noon-11pm Mon, to midnight Tue-Sat, to 10pm Sun; 7, 86, M M4 Szent Gellért tér, 18, 19, 47, 49)

Entertainment

Fonó Buda Music House

LIVE MUSIC

14 MAP P56, C8

This venue has *táncház* (folk music and dance) programs several times a week, especially on Wednesday at 6.30pm and Friday at 8pm, as well as concerts by big-name bands (mostly playing world music) throughout the month; it's one of the best venues in town for this sort of thing. Consult the website for more details. (Fonó Budai Zeneház; 1-206 5300; www.fono.hu; XI Sztregova utca 3; box office 9am-5pm Mon-Fri; 17, 41, 47, 56)

A38

LIVE MUSIC

15 MAP P56, F7

Moored on the Buda side just south of Petőfi Bridge, the A38 is a decommissioned Ukrainian stone hauler from 1968 that has been recycled as a major live-music venue. It's so cool that Lonely Planet readers once voted it the best bar in the world. The ship's hold rocks throughout the year. Terraces open in the warmer weather. (box office 1-464 3940; www.a38.hu; XI Petőfi híd & Henryk Sławik rakpart; 11am-midnight Sun-Thu, to 3am Fri & Sat; 212, 4, 6)

A38

Shopping

Prezent

DESIGN

16 MAP P56, B2

This shop specialising in 'sustainable Hungarian design' sells fashion and accessories as well as natural cosmetics. Earnest and admirable and very high-quality stuff too! (www.prezentbudapest.hu; I Döbrentei utca 16; 10.30am-7pm; 18, 19, 41)

Chocofacture

CHOCOLATE

17 MAP P56, D6

Some people say the chocolate this small shop makes is the best in town. Handmade bonbons are filled with fresh ingredients (fig, berries, white cheese) and/or wine and *pálinka*. Gift boxes can be personalised. (06 30 230 2068; XI Kende utca 3; 10am-5pm Mon & Sat, 9am-6pm Tue-Fri; M M4 Móricz Zsigmond körtér, 18, 19, 47, 49)

Worth a Trip

Memento Park

The socialist Disneyland of Memento Park, 10km southwest of the city centre, has more than 40 statues, busts and plaques of Lenin, Marx, Engels, home-grown heroes such as Béla Kun, superhuman workers and others whose likenesses have ended up in dustbins or on rubbish heaps in other countries of the region. It offers an extraordinary view into the lost face of communist Hungary dating back a mere three decades.

☎ 1-424 7500

www.mementopark.hu

XXII Balatoni út & Szabadkai utca

adult/student 1500/1200Ft

🕒 10am-dusk

🚌 101B, 101E, 150

The Monuments

Ogle the socialist realism and try to imagine that at least four of these monstrous relics were erected as recently as the late 1980s; a few of them, including the Béla Kun memorial of 'our hero' in a crowd by fence-sitting sculptor Imre Varga, were still in place as late as 1992.

Old Barrack Exhibition

An exhibition centre in an old barracks – Hungary was called 'the happiest barrack in the camp' under communism – has displays on the events of 1956 and the changes since 1989, as well as documentary film with rare footage of secret agents collecting information on 'subversives'. The Communist Hotline allows you to listen in on the likes of Lenin, Stalin and even Che Guevara in conversation.

Stalin's Boots

Excellent selfie ops include the reproduced remains of Stalin's boots (left after a crowd pulled the statue down from its plinth on XIV Dózsa György út during the 1956 Uprising) and an original two-stroke Trabant 601, the 'people's car' produced in East Germany, and popular throughout the Soviet bloc.

The Shop

We normally don't recommend museum gift shops, but this one is a treasure trove of kitsch communist memorabilia: pins, CDs of revolutionary songs, books and posters.

★ Top Tips

- If you go via public bus 150 the park website offers a Memento Park Bonus Tour of sights to follow along the way.
- English-language tours (1200Ft) of the park lasting 50 minutes depart daily from the main entrance at 11.45am and at other times too in high season (May to October).

Take a Break

Catering facilities are nonexistent at the park. Before you set out take a picnic or eat at one of the places in south Buda near the M4, such as the Kelet Cafe & Gallery (p61).

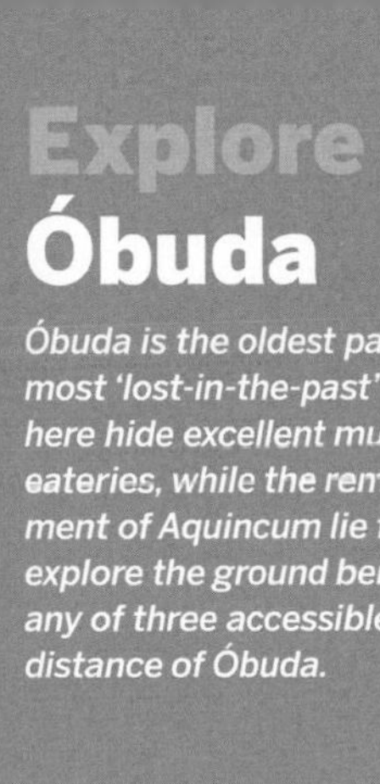

Explore Óbuda

Óbuda is the oldest part of Buda and retains an almost 'lost-in-the-past' village feel. The narrow streets here hide excellent museums and some legendary eateries, while the remains of the Roman settlement of Aquincum lie further north. Adventurers can explore the ground beneath the city by venturing into any of three accessible caves within easy striking distance of Óbuda.

The Short List

- ***Pálvölgy Cave (p70)*** *Exploring the world beneath you by visiting the most spectacular yet still accessible of the three nearby caves.*
- ***Vasarely Museum (p70)*** *Spacing out while viewing the truly mind-blowing works of op art at the artist's eponymous museum.*
- ***Béla Bartók Memorial House (p72)*** *Enjoying Bartók's music in the very place of its birth by attending a classical music recital.*

Getting There & Around

Bus 109 from II Batthyány tér to Óbuda. Buses 34 and 106 from III Szentlélek tér to Aquincum.

Tram 1 runs along XIII Róbert Károly körút from City Park to Árpád Bridge in Óbuda. Trams 17, 19 and 41 link III Bécsi út with II Margit körút and Gellért Hill.

(HÉV) The H5 serves Szentlélek tér and Tímár utca stops in Óbuda as well as Aquincum.

Óbuda Map on p68

Vasarely Museum (p70) LIUB SHTEIN / SHUTTERSTOCK ©

A
B
C
D
E
F
1
2
3
4
Hajógyári-sziget (Óbuda Island)
Fő tér
12
Szentlélek tér
Vasarely Museum
2
Szentlélek tér
Árpád-híd
ÓBUDA
Vörösvári út
Flórián tér
Serfőző u
Korona tér
1
Hungarian Museum of Trade & Tourism
14
10
Kis Korona u
Mókus u
Goldberger Leó u
Perc u
Fényes Adolf u
Lajos u
Tímár u
Textilgyár u
Árpád fejedelem út
Pacsirtamező u
8
Nagyszombat u
Lajos u
Csemete u
9
Bokor u
Bécsi út
ÚJLAK
Viador u
Beszterce u
Zápor u
Szőlő u
Dévai Bíró M tér
Kiscelli u
Reménység u
Föld u
San Marco u
Kenyeres u
Selmeci u
Tégla u
REMETEHEGY
Kiscell Museum
6
Kolostor út
Doberdó út
MÁTYÁSHEGY
Folyondár u
Remetehegyi út
Remete köz
Nyereg út
Mátyás-hegy
3
Pálvölgy Cave
Mátyáshegyi út
Virág Benedek u
Szépvölgyi út
Felső Zöldmáli út
13

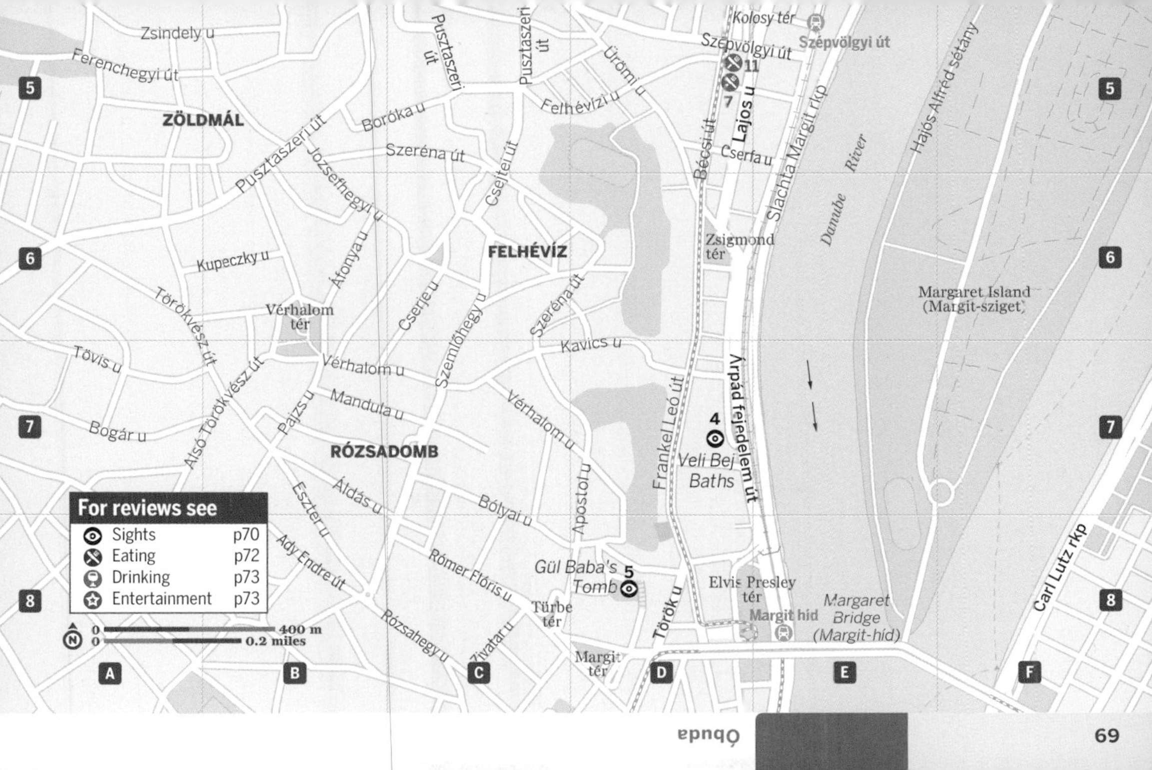

Kolosy tér
Szépvölgyi út
Szépvölgyi út
Zsindely u
Ferenchegyi út
Pusztaszeri út
Pusztaszeri út
Ürömi u
Felhévízi u
Lajos u
Bécsi út
Cserfa u
Slachta Margit rkp
Hajós Alfréd sétány
Danube River
ZÖLDMÁL
Boróka u
Szeréna út
Pusztaszeri út
Józsefhegyi u
Cseitei út
FELHÉVÍZ
Zsigmond tér
Kupeczky u
Áfonya u
Cserje u
Szemlőhegy u
Szeréna út
Margaret Island (Margit-sziget)
Vérhalom tér
Törökvész út
Kavics u
Tövis u
Vérhalom u
Alsó Törökvész út
Pajzs u
Mandula u
Vérhalom u
Frankel Leó út
Árpád fejedelem út
4
Veli Bej Baths
Bogár u
RÓZSADOMB
Eszter u
Áldás u
Bólyai u
Apostol u
Ady Endre út
Rómer Flóris u
Gül Baba's Tomb
5
Elvis Presley tér
Margit híd
Margaret Bridge (Margit-híd)
Carl Lutz rkp
Türbe tér
Rózsahegy u
Zivatar u
Török u
Margit tér
11
7
For reviews see
Sights p70
Eating p72
Drinking p73
Entertainment p73
0 400 m
0 0.2 miles
A
B
C
D
E
F
5
6
7
8

Sights

Hungarian Museum of Trade & Tourism

MUSEUM

1 MAP P68, E2

This superb museum traces Budapest's catering and hospitality trade through the ages, including the dramatic changes after WWII, with restaurant items, tableware, advertising posters, packaging, original shop signs and advertising. There's also an intimate look at the lives of various tradespeople – from pastry chefs and publicans to hoteliers and launderers. Go upstairs for some cutting-edge temporary exhibits. A gem. (Magyar Kereskedelmi és Vendéglátó-ipari Múzeum; 1-375 6249; www.mkvm.hu; III Korona tér 1; adult/student 1000/500Ft; 10am-6pm Tue-Sun; 29, 109, (HÉV) H5 Tímár utca)

Vasarely Museum

GALLERY

2 MAP P68, F1

Installed in the imposing Zichy Mansion (Zichy kastély), built in 1757, this renovated and rehung gallery contains some 150 works by Victor Vasarely (or Vásárhelyi Győző, as he was known before he emigrated to Paris in 1930), the late 'father of op art'. Op art is short for 'optical art', a style of abstract visual art that uses optical illusions. Watch his excellent works like *Ibadan-Pos* (1977) and *Keek* (1980) as they 'swell' and 'move' around the canvas. (Vasarely Múzeum; 1-388 7551; www.vasarely.hu; III Szentlélek tér 6; adult/6-26yr 800/400Ft; 10am-6pm Tue-Sun; 29, 109, 1, Szentlélek tér)

Pálvölgy Cave

CAVE

3 MAP P68, A3

This 29km-long cave – the second-largest in Hungary – was discovered in 1904 and is noted for both its spectacular stalactites and rock formations. Tours last an hour and depart from 10.15am (last tour at 4.15pm) from the lowest level, taking you through dank, claustrophobia-inducing passages and up several hundred steps. Highlights include John's Lookout in the largest of chambers, as well as Radium Hall, reminiscent of Dante's *Inferno*. The temperature is a constant 11°C, so wear a jacket or jumper. (Pálvölgyi-barlang; 1-325 9505; www.dunaipoly.hu/en/places/interpretation-sites/pal-volgyi-cave; II Szépvölgyi út 162/a; adult/concession 1400/1100Ft, joint ticket with Szemlőhegy Cave 2000/1600Ft; 10am-4pm Tue-Sun; 65)

Veli Bej Baths

BATHHOUSE

4 MAP P68, D7

Veli Bej Baths is one of the oldest (1575) and most beautiful Ottoman-era baths in Budapest, with five thermal pools of varying temperatures – the central pool lies under a lovely cupola. The water is high in sodium, potassium and calcium, and good for joint ailments, chronic arthritis and calcium deficiency. There's also a cluster of saunas and steam rooms; massage available. (Veli Bej Fürdője; ☎1-438 8587; www.irgalmasrend.hu/site/velibej/sprachen/en; II Árpád fejedelem útja 7; 6am-noon 2240Ft, 3-7pm 2800Ft, after 7pm 2240Ft; ⏰6am-noon & 3-9pm; 🚌9, 109, 🚋4, 6, 17, 19)

Gül Baba's Tomb — ISLAMIC TOMB

5 MAP P68, D8

This renovated tomb contains the mortal remains of one Gül Baba, an Ottoman dervish who took part in the capture of Buda in 1541 and is known in Hungary as the 'Father of Roses'. The tomb/mosque (1548) is a pilgrimage place for Muslims, especially from Turkey, and you must remove your shoes before entering. (Gül Baba türbéje; ☎1-237 4400; www.museum.hu/budapest/gulbabaturbe; II Türbe tér 1; admission free; ⏰10am-6pm; 🚋4, 6, 17)

Kiscell Museum — MUSEUM

6 MAP P68, C2

Housed in an 18th-century monastery, this museum contains three excellent sections. Downstairs you'll find a complete 19th-century apothecary brought from Kálvin tér; a wonderful assembly of ancient signboards advertising shops and other trades; and rooms dressed in empire, Biedermeier and art nouveau furniture. An impressive collection of works by artists József Rippl-Rónai, Lajos Tihanyi, István Csók and Béla Czóbel, and organised by the **Municipal Picture Gallery** (Fővárosi Képtár), is upstairs. The stark Gothic church shell used

Gül Baba's Tomb

Béla Bartók Memorial House

North of Szilágyi Erzsébet fasor, this 1924 **house** (Bartók Béla Emlékház; 1-394 2100; www.bartokmuseum.hu; II Csalán út 29; adult/concession 1600/800Ft; 10am-5pm Tue-Sun; 5, 29, 61) is where the great composer resided from 1932 until 1940, when he emigrated to the USA. Visits are by guided tour and include seeing the old Edison recorder (complete with wax cylinders) that Bartók used to record Hungarian folk music in Transylvania, as well as his beloved hand-carved dining-room furniture and even half a cigarette he smoked! Chamber-music concerts take place here throughout the year; see the website for details.

for temporary multimedia and art exhibits is visually arresting. (Kiscelli Múzeum; 06 20 544 1348, 1-368 7971; www.kiscellimuzeum.hu; III Kiscelli utca 108; adult/concession 1600/800Ft; 10am-6pm Tue-Sun Apr-Oct, to 4pm Tue-Sun Nov-Mar; 29, 109, 165, 17, 19, 41)

Eating

Chefparade Cafe

CAFE €

7 MAP P68, D5

This place, run by a **cooking school** (06 20 316 1876, 1-210 6042; www.chefparade.hu; II Bécsi út 27; 8am-5pm Mon-Thu, to 4pm Fri), is a great place to pop in for lunch, with shop-made soups, sandwiches, quiche and cakes. (06 20 473 7817; www.chefparade.hu; II Bécsi út 27; soups & sandwiches 490-790Ft; 11.45am-2pm; 17, 19, 41)

Pastrami

INTERNATIONAL €

8 MAP P68, E3

In Óbuda's Újlak district, this light, bright bistro-meets-New-York-style-deli does indeed serve its namesake in its many guises, including the celebrated Reuben sandwich (2900Ft). But come here also for breakfast, and more complicated mains, such as pumpkin risotto or duck confit with horseradish potatoes. (1-430 1731; www.pastrami.hu; III Lajos utca 93-99; mains 2100-4900Ft; 8am-11pm; 17, 19, 41, (HÉV) H5 Tímár utca)

Sushi Sei

JAPANESE €€

9 MAP P68, D4

This stylish restaurant is one of the best spots in Budapest for a wide spectrum of authentic Japanese cuisine. Apart from beautifully presented nigiri, sushi and tempura sets, you can feast on cold soba noodles, yakitori, tonkatsu and grilled fish. The bento sets are 9800Ft to 10,800Ft, bento lunch boxes a mere 3000Ft. (06 30 435 0567, 1-240 4065; www.sushisei.hu; III Bécsi út 58; mains 2600-6300Ft; noon-10pm Sun-Thu, to 11pm Fri & Sat; 17, 19, 41)

Kéhli Vendéglő HUNGARIAN €€

10 MAP P68, E2

Self-consciously rustic, Kéhli has some of the best Hungarian food in town. One of Hungary's best-loved writers, the novelist Gyula Krúdy (1878–1933), who lived in nearby III Korona tér, moonlighted as a restaurant critic and enjoyed the *forró velőscsont fokhagymás pirítóssal* (bone marrow with garlic on toast; 990Ft) so much that he included it in one of his novels. (1-368 0613; www.kehli.hu; III Mókus utca 22; mains 1590-6990Ft; noon-midnight; 29, 109, (HÉV) H5 Tímár utca)

Földes Józsi Konyhája HUNGARIAN €€

11 MAP P68, D5

In a lovely old town house, this rustic place established by former hotel chef Joe Earthy some years back still serves excellent Hungarian homestyle dishes, including veal stew with dumplings (2750Ft) and a good range of *főzelék* (vegetables in a roux; 850Ft). Lovely garden seating in the warmer months too. (06 70 500 0222; www.foldesjozsikonyhaja.hu; II Bécsi út 31; mains 2100-4400Ft; 11.30am-3.30pm Mon, 11.30am-4pm & 6-10pm Tue-Sun; 4, 6, 17)

Új Sípos Halászkert HUNGARIAN €€

12 MAP P68, F1

This old-style eatery faces Óbuda's most beautiful and historical square. Try the signature *halászlé* (fish soup; from 1190Ft), which comes in various guises. As the restaurant's motto says: *Halászlében verhetetlen* (You can't beat fish soup). Several vegetarian options too, and there's a children's menu. (New Piper Fisher's Garden; 1-388 8745; www.ujsipos.hu; III Fő tér 6; mains 1290-6790Ft; noon-10pm Sun-Thu, to 11pm Fri, to midnight Sat; ; 29, 109, (HÉV) H5 Szentlélek tér)

Drinking

Daubner Cukrászda CAFE

13 MAP P68, C4

People come to this place dating from 1901 for its macarons, traditional Hungarian cakes and *pogácsa* (savoury scone). You can also enjoy a coffee and cake in the minimalist cafe, but it's worth the trip to buy one of the best slices of cake – try the sour-cherry *pite* (400Ft) or *flódni* (520Ft) – in town. (06 20 329 8952, 1-335 2253; www.daubnercukraszda.hu; II Szépvölgyi út 50; cakes 380-530Ft; 9am-7pm Tue-Sun; 29, 65)

Entertainment

Óbuda Society CONCERT VENUE

14 MAP P68, E2

This very intimate venue in Óbuda takes its music seriously and hosts recitals and some chamber orchestras. Highly recommended. (Óbudai Társaskör; 1-250 0288; www.obudaitarsaskor.hu; III Kis Korona utca 7; tickets 1000-2400Ft; 86, Tímár utca)

Worth a Trip

Aquincum

Aquincum, dating from the end of the 1st century AD and the most complete Roman civilian town in Hungary, had paved streets and sumptuous single-storey houses, complete with courtyards, fountains and mosaic floors, as well as sophisticated drainage and heating systems. It's not all immediately apparent as you explore the ruins in the open-air archaeological park, but the museum helps put it all in perspective.

www.aquincum.hu

III Szentendrei út 135

adult/concession museum & park 1600/800Ft, park only Apr-Oct 1000/500Ft

museum 10am-6pm Tue-Sun Apr-Oct, to 4pm Nov-Mar, park 9am-6pm Tue-Sun Apr-Oct

34, 106, (HÉV) H5 Aquincum

Mithraism

Mithraism, the worship of the god Mithra, originated in Persia. As Roman rule extended into Asia, the religion became extremely popular with traders, imperial slaves and mercenaries of the Roman army, and spread rapidly throughout the empire in the 2nd and 3rd centuries AD. It was the principal rival of Christianity, because of the striking similarity in many of their rituals, until Constantine came to the throne in the 4th century.

Aquincum Museum

The museum ('exhibition hall' on the map) lies just north of the entrance to the Roman town. It contains an impressive collection of household objects: pottery, weaponry, grooming implements, a military discharge diploma... In the basement there are some hokey virtual games for kids, such as battling with a gladiator. Look out for the replica of a 3rd-century portable organ called a hydra, the mock-up of a Roman bath and a copy of a road map of the Roman Empire *(Tabula Peutingeriana)*.

Painter's House & Mithraeum

Just opposite the museum is the wonderful Painter's House, a recreated and furnished Roman dwelling from the 3rd century AD. Behind it is the Symphorus Mithraeum, a temple dedicated to the god Mithra.

Main Thoroughfare

Just north of the museum, the arrow-straight main thoroughfare leads you past ruins of the large public bath with mosaic, the *macellum* (market) and the *basilica* (courthouse). Most of the large stone sculptures and sarcophagi are in the old museum building to the northeast.

★ Top Tips

- If you are travelling to Aquincum on the HÉV suburban train, view the **Roman Civilian Amphitheatre** (Római polgári amfiteátrum; III Zsófia utca & Szentendrei ut; admission free; (HÉV) H5 Aquincum) first before crossing busy III Szentendrei út.
- Tickets to the Castle Museum (Budapest History Museum) or Kiscell Museum are valid here for 30 days.

Take a Break

A branch of the popular **Nagyi Palacsintázója** (1-368 9257; https://nagyipali.hu; III Szentendrei út 131; pancakes 320-990Ft; 11am-1.45am; 34, 106, (HÉV) H5 Aquincum) pancake chain is just south of the museum.

Walking Tour

Touring the Buda Hills

Visitors to Budapest head for the hills – the city's green 'lungs' – for a variety of reasons. There's great hiking, a couple of trip-worthy sights and activities, and the summer homes of well-heeled Budapest families to ogle. But locals come just to ride the unusual forms of transport on offer. It really can be said that getting to/from the Buda Hills is half the fun.

Getting There

M M2 Széll Kálmán tér.

59 or 61 to the Cog Railway lower terminus.

291 from the Chairlift upper terminus to II Szilágyi Erzsébet fasor.

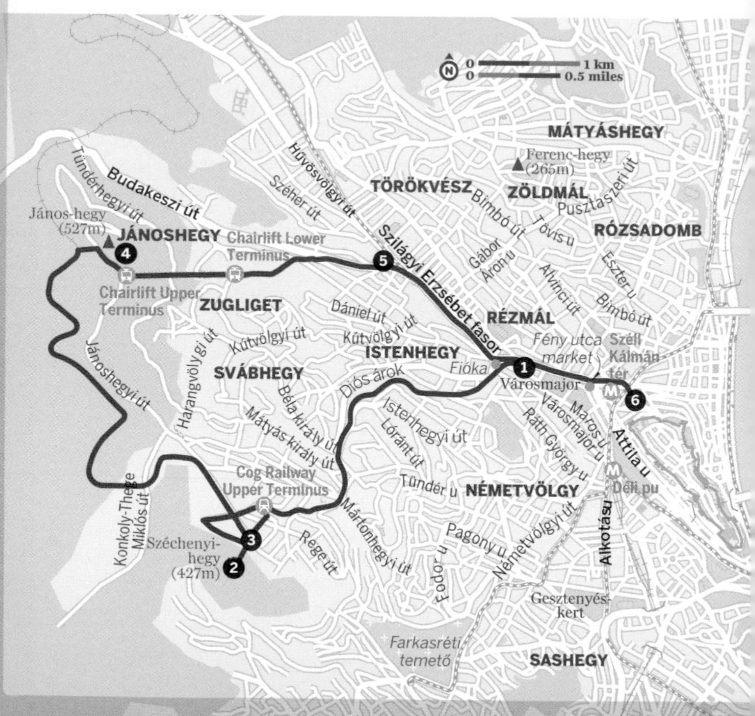

❶ Going Up

From Széll Kálmán tér metro station, walk west along Szilágyi Erzsébet fasor for 10 minutes (or take tram 56 or 61 for two stops) to the lower terminus of the **Cog Railway** (Fogaskerekű vasút; www.bkv.hu; XII Szilágyi Erzsébet fasor 14-16; admission 1 BKV ticket or 350Ft; ⏲5am-11pm) just opposite the circular Hotel Budapest at No 47. Built in 1874, the railway climbs for 3.7km in 14 minutes two to five times an hour to Széchenyi-hegy (427m).

❷ Children's Railway

Just south of the Széchenyi-hegy station on XII Hegyhát út is the narrow-gauge **Children's Railway** (Gyermekvasút; ☎1-397 5394; www.gyermekvasut.hu; adult/child one way 800/400Ft, return or with stopover 1400/700Ft; ⏲9am-5.30pm Tue-Fri, to 6pm Sat & Sun Mar-Oct, varies in other months). Built in 1951 by Pioneers (socialist Scouts) and now staffed entirely by schoolchildren aged 10 to 14 (the engineer excluded), the little train chugs along for 11km, terminating at Hűvösvölgy 45 minutes later.

❸ Elizabeth Lookout

Trails fan out from any of the nine stations of the railway line or you can return to Széll Kálmán tér on tram 61 from Hűvösvölgy. Better still, disembark at János-hegy, the fourth stop and the highest point (527m) in the hills. From atop the 23.5m-tall **Elizabeth Lookout** (Erzsébet-kilátó; Erzsébet kilátó utca; ⏲8am-8pm; Children's Railway to János-hegy), with 134 steps, you can see the Tatra Mountains in Slovakia.

❹ Going Down

About 700m to the east of the tower is the **Chairlift** (Libegő; www.bkv.hu; one way/return adult 1000/1400Ft, 6-26yr 600/800Ft; ⏲10am-7pm May-Aug, varies rest of year; 291), which will take you 1040m down at 4km/h to XII Zugligeti út. From here bus 291 will take you to Nyugati station via Margaret Bridge.

❺ Dinner in the Hills

Bus 291 stops right in front of **Szép Ilona** (☎1-275 1392; www.szepilonavendeglo.hu; II Budakeszi út 1-3; mains 1700-5800Ft; ⏲noon-10pm; 56, 61), a Buda Hills eatery that is the place to come for hearty indigenous fare. But if you'd like something a bit more, well, 21st century, a bistro and wine bar called **Fióka** (☎1-426 5555; www.facebook.com/fiokavarosmajor; XII Városmajor utca 75; mains 2950-6850Ft; ⏲11am-midnight Wed-Sun; 56, 59, 61) is almost next to the Cog Railway's lower terminus.

❻ Nightcap

Stop for a drink or two at **Oscar American Bar** (p47) just up from II Széll Kálmán tér on the way to Castle Hill.

50%

Explore

Belváros

The 'Inner Town', the most heavily visited part of Pest, is where you'll find Váci utca, with its luxury shops, restaurants and bars, and Vörösmarty tér, home to the city's most celebrated cukrászda (cake shop) and the first of its four Michelin-starred restaurants. The centre is Deák Ferenc tér, the main square where three of the four metro lines converge.

The Short List

- ***Váci utca (p80)*** *Strolling up the epicentre of Budapest tourism, taking in its unusual architecture and fine shops.*
- ***Gerbeaud (p81)*** *Savouring a cup of something warm and a slice of something sweet at Budapest's finest cukrászda (cake shop).*
- ***Pesti Vigadó (p84)*** *Climbing the grand staircase of this remarkable 19th-century building and enjoying the views from the terrace.*
- ***Baraka (p86)*** *Treating yourself to one of the finest meals in town at this upscale, experimental restaurant.*

Getting There & Around

M M1 Vörösmarty tér, M3 Ferenciek tere, M1/2/3 Deák Ferenc tér, M3/4 Kálvin tér.

Tram 47 or 49 from V Deák Ferenc tér to Liberty Bridge, 2 from Belgrád rakpart to V Szent István körút.

Bus V Ferenciek tere for 7, 8E or 110 to Buda; V Egyetem tér for 15 or 115 to IX Boráros tér.

Belváros Map on p82

Gerbeaud (p81) RAINER MARTINI / LOOK-FOTO / GETTY IMAGES ©

Walking Tour

Exploring Váci Utca & Vörösmarty Tér

The capital's premier shopping street, Váci utca is a pedestrian strip crammed largely with chain stores, touristy restaurants and a smattering of shops and notable buildings worth seeking out. It was the total length of the city of Pest in the Middle Ages.

Getting There

M M1/2/3 Deák Ferenc tér, M3 Ferenciek tere

2, 47, 48, 49

5, 7, 110

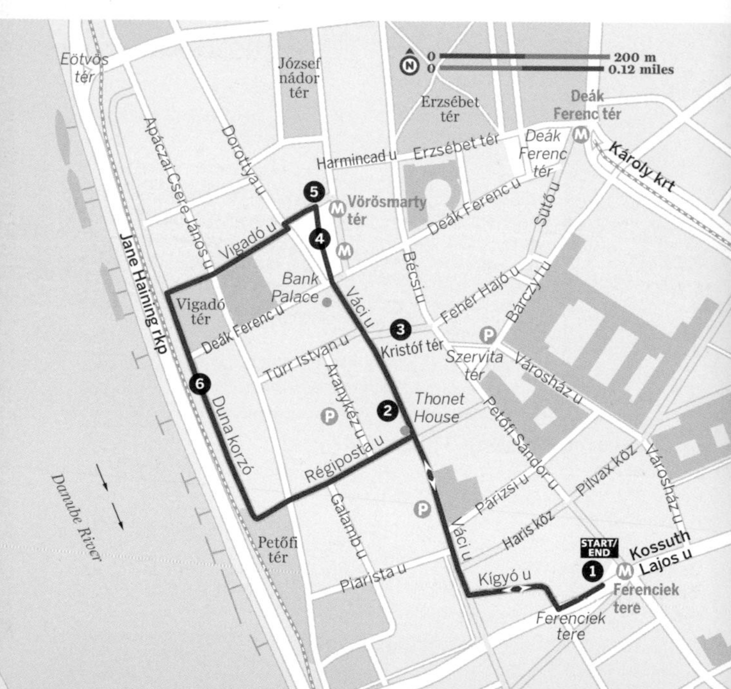

❶ Párisi Udvar

A good place to start is at the **Párisi Udvar** (Parisian Court, Brudern House; V Ferenciek tere 5; M M3 Ferenciek tere), built in 1909. It was under renovation at the time of writing, but you should be able to get a glimpse of the interior and its ornately decorated ceiling once it opens as a 130-room hotel. Váci utca is immediately to the west.

❷ Philanthia

Head first to **Philanthia** (☎06 70 933 2266; www.facebook.com/LikePhilanthia; V Váci utca 9; ⏲10am-7pm Mon-Sat, to 6pm Sun; M M1/2/3 Deák Ferenc tér, 2), which has an original (and very rare) art nouveau interior from 1906. Nearby **Thonet House** (V Váci utca 11/a; M M1/2/3 Deák Ferenc tér, 2) is a masterpiece built by Ödön Lechner in 1890, and to the west, at Régiposta utca 13, there's a ceramic relief of an old postal coach by the celebrated ceramicist Margit Kovács of Szentendre.

❸ Fishergirl Fountain

Just off the top of Váci utca in Kristóf tér is the little **Fishergirl Statue** (V Kristóf tér; M M1 Vörösmarty tér), dating from the 19th century and complete with a ship's wheel behind her that actually turns. A short distance to the northwest is the sumptuous **Bank Palace** (Bank Palota; V Deák Ferenc utca 3-5; M M1 Vörösmarty tér), built in 1915 and once the home of the Budapest Stock Exchange. It has since been converted into a shopping gallery called Váci 1; the Hard Rock Cafe Budapest is the anchor tenant.

❹ Vörösmarty Tér

Váci utca disgorges into **Vörösmarty tér** (M M1 Vörösmarty tér), a large square of smart shops, galleries, cafes and an artist or two, who will draw your portrait or caricature. In the centre is a statue of Mihály Vörösmarty, the 19th-century poet after whom the square is named.

❺ Cake Stop

At the northern end of the square is **Gerbeaud** (☎1-429 9000; www.gerbeaud.hu; V Vörösmarty tér 7-8; ⏲9am-9pm; M M1 Vörösmarty tér), Budapest's fanciest and most famous cafe and cake shop. Grab a seat on the terrace and don't fail to order the *Dobos torta,* a scrumptious seven-layer chocolate buttercream cake with a caramelised brown sugar top invented by the Hungarian confectioner József C Dobos in 1884.

❻ Danube Promenade

A pleasant way to return to Ferenciek tere is along the **Duna korzó** (M M1 Vörösmarty tér, 2), the riverside 'Danube Promenade' between Chain and Elizabeth Bridges.

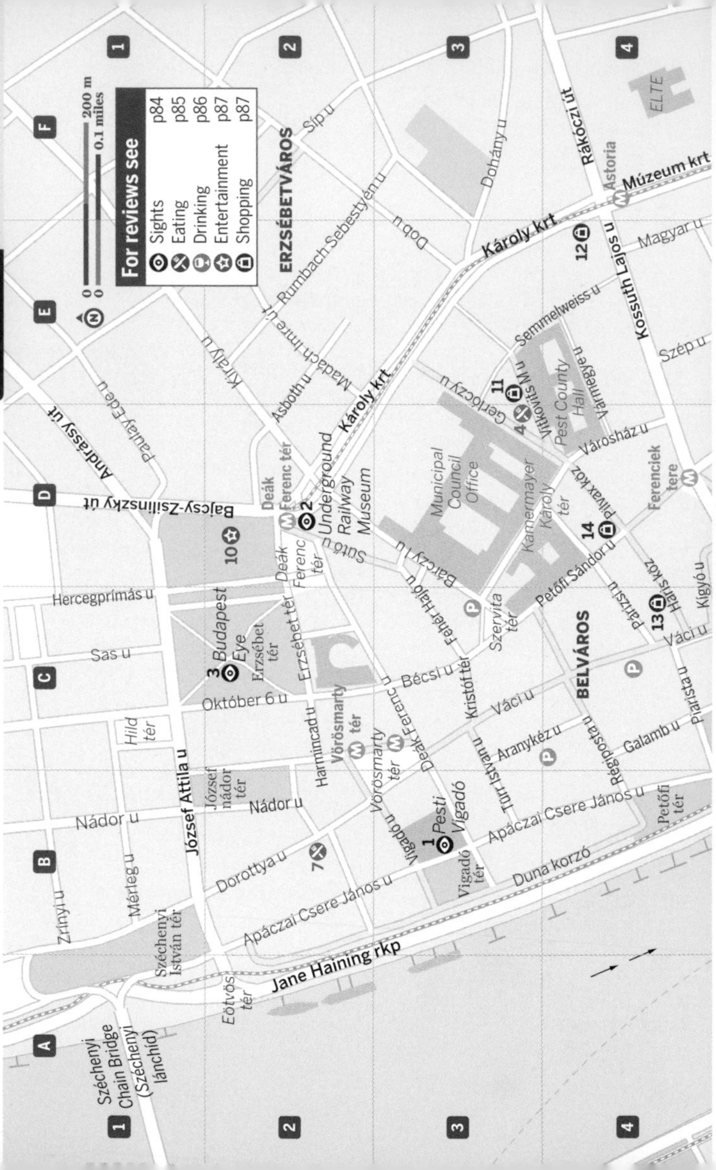

For reviews see

Sights	p84
Eating	p85
Drinking	p86
Entertainment	p87
Shopping	p87

0 200 m
0 0.1 miles

A B C D E F
1 2 3 4

ERZSÉBETVÁROS
BELVÁROS
Széchenyi Chain Bridge (Széchenyi lánchíd)
Széchenyi István tér
Eötvös tér
Jane Haining rkp
Zrínyi u
Mérleg u
Nádor u
József Attila u
Hild tér
Sas u
Hercegprímás u
Bajcsy-Zsilinszky út
Andrássy út
Paulay Ede u
Király u
Asboth u
Madách Imre út
Rumbach Sebestyén u
Síp u
Dob u
Dohány u
Rákóczi út
Astoria
Múzeum krt
Károly krt
ELTE
Magyar u
Kossuth Lajos u
Szép u
Semmelweiss u
Vármegye u
Pest County Hall
Vitkovits M u
Gerlóczy u
Városház u
Ferenciek tere
Pilvax köz
Károly tér
Kamermayer
Municipal Council Office
Barczy u
Sütő u
Deák Ferenc tér
Deák Ferenc tér
Underground Railway Museum
10
3 Budapest Eye
Erzsébet tér
Erzsébet tér
Október 6 u
József nádor tér
Nádor u
Dorottya u
7
Apáczai Csere János u
Harmincad u
Vörösmarty tér
Vörösmarty tér
Deák Ferenc u
Vigadó u
1 Pesti Vigadó
Vigadó tér
Duna korzó
Türr István u
Bécsi u
Kristóf tér
Fehér Hajó u
Szervita tér
Petőfi Sándor u
14
Párizsi u
13
Haris köz
Kígyó u
Váci u
Váci u
Aranykéz u
Régiposta u
Galamb u
Piarista u
Petőfi tér
Apáczai Csere János u
11
4
12

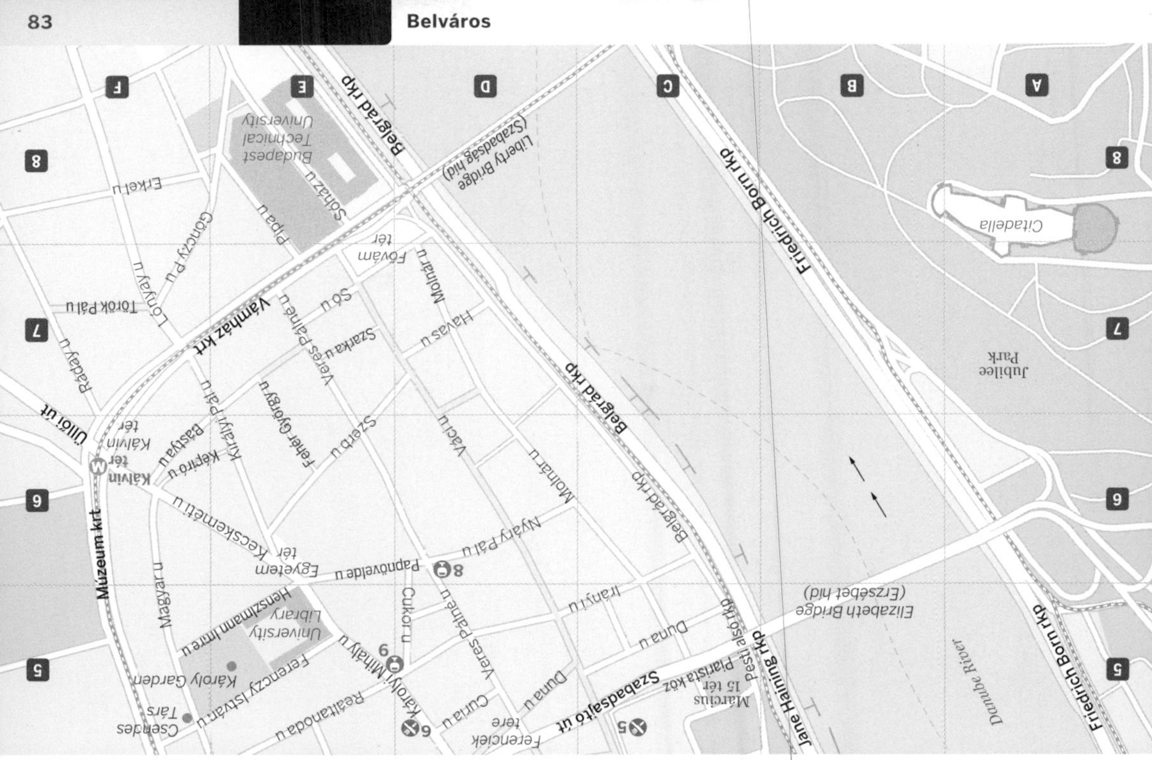
Múzeum krt
Üllői út
Kálvin tér
Ráday u
Török Pál u
Lónyay u
Erkel u
Gönczy P u
Budapest Technical University
Pipa u
Sóház u
Vámház krt
Belgrád rkp
Fővám tér
Só u
Szarka u
Veres Pálné u
Fehér György u
Királyi Pál u
Képíró u
Bástya u
Kecskeméti u
Magyar u
Csendes Társ
Károly Garden
Ferenczy István u
Henszlmann Imre u
University Library
Egyetem tér
Papnövelde u
Károlyi Mihály u
Reáltanoda u
Cukor u
Szerb u
Váci u
Havas u
Molnár u
Nyáry Pál u
Liberty Bridge (Szabadság híd)
Curia u
Ferenciek tere
Duna u
Irányi u
Szabadsajtó út
Március 15 tér
Piarista köz
Pesti alsó rkp
Jane Haining rkp
Elizabeth Bridge (Erzsébet híd)
Danube River
Friedrich Born rkp
Jubilee Park
Citadella
A
B
C
D
E
F
5
6
7
8

Sights

Pesti Vigadó

NOTABLE BUILDING

1 MAP P82, B3

This Romantic-style concert hall, built in 1865 but badly damaged during WWII, faces the river to the west of Vörösmarty tér. Reopened in 2014 after a massive reconstruction, the building has been fully restored to its former grandeur. Floors 5 and 6 have been set aside for temporary exhibitions, and there's now a fantastic terrace with a small cafe affording expansive views over the Danube. It's a fantastic place to catch a classical concert in glamorous surrounds. (Pest Concert Hall; 1-328 3300; www.vigado.hu; V Vigadó tér 2; adult/concession combined ticket 2500/1250Ft, 'walking' ticket with no exhibits 1400/700Ft; 10am-7pm; M M1 Vörösmarty tér, 2)

A Different View

A lovely way to see the Belváros from a different angle altogether is to hop on one of the **BKV passenger ferries** that make stops along the Danube. Board the D11 or D 12 at IX Boráros tér, from where the ferry crosses to the opposite bank and then returns to Pest; get back on dry land at V Petőfi tér, or stay on for stops up to Margaret Island and beyond.

Underground Railway Museum

MUSEUM

2 MAP P82, D2

In the pedestrian subway/underpass below V Deák Ferenc tér, with its entrance within the main ticket office, the small, revamped Underground Railway Museum traces the development of the capital's underground lines. Much emphasis is put on the little yellow metro (M1), continental Europe's first underground railway, which opened for the millennary celebrations in 1896. The museum is atmospherically housed in a stretch of tunnel and station, and features wonderfully restored carriages. (Földalatti Vasúti Múzeum; www.bkv.hu/en/millennium_underground_museum; Deák Ferenc tér metro station; adult/concession 350/280Ft; 10am-5pm Tue-Sun; M M1/2/3 Deák Ferenc tér)

Budapest Eye

AMUSEMENT PARK

3 MAP P82, C2

Dominating V Erzsébet tér, the attraction exaggerates just a titch when it claims 'The Budapest Eye is to Budapest what the London Eye is to London'. Huh? At just 65m, it's less than half the height of London's wheel and the ride is over in three twirls. Still, it does offer stunning panoramic views of Pest and across the Danube to Buda, and is particularly impressive at night. (Oriaskerek; 06 70 636 0629; www.oriaskerek.com; V Erzsébet tér; adult/child/family 2700/1500/6900Ft, fast-track ticket

3300Ft; ⌚10am-11pm Mon & Tue, to midnight Sun, Wed & Thu, to 1am Fri & Sat; M M1/2/3 Deák Ferenc tér)

Eating

Impostor

ASIAN €€

4 MAP P82, D3

Now in a new, more central location, elegant Impostor serves hybrid dishes that echo the owners' passion for Asia and Latin America. Though there are more elaborate main courses on offer, we come for the delectable (and quite inspired) mixed dumplings (1350Ft) and *bao* (steamed, filled rice-flour buns; 1490Ft to 1990Ft). (☎06 30 505 3632; http://impostor.hu/impostor; V Vitkovits Mihály 8; mains 2990-3690Ft; ⌚noon-10pm Mon-Thu, to midnight Fri & Sat; M M1/2/3 Deák Ferenc tér, 🚋47, 49)

Monk's Bistrot

HUNGARIAN €€

5 MAP P82, C5

With its vaguely industrial decor, an open kitchen and hip serving staff, this ambitious restaurant specialises in bold pairings of ingredients that nevertheless seem to work, alongside contemporary reimaginings of Hungarian dishes. The goat cheese with peaches really shines, a s does the pike-perch with bergamot and dill. Weekday three-course lunch is a bargain at 2780Ft. (☎06 30 789 4718; http://english.monks.hu; V Piarista köz 1; mains 3880-6780Ft; ⌚11am-11pm; 🚋2)

Pesti Vigadó

Károly Garden

A pleasant place to take a breather, flora-filled **Károly Garden** (Károlyi kert; Map p82, E5; V Ferenczy István utca; M M2 Astoria, 47, 48, 49) was built for the Károly Palace, which now houses a literature museum. Frequented by locals, many with families – it has a lovely little playground – the garden is a riot of colourful flowerbeds in the summer months, and there are plenty of shady benches. **Csendes Társ** (Map p82, F5; 1-727 2100; V Magyar utca 18; 11am-11pm; M M2 Astoria, 47, 49) is an atmospheric spot for a sundowner or snack, with a little terrace of tables around the park's entrance gate.

Kárpátia

HUNGARIAN **€€**

6 MAP P82, D5

A fin-de-siècle palace dating from 1877, the 'Carpathia' serves almost-modern Hungarian and Transylvanian specialities in both a palatial restaurant in the back and a less-expensive *söröző* (brasserie). The mostly meaty dishes are expertly prepared and the Hungarian wine list is solid. This is one place to hear authentic *csárdás* (Gypsy-style folk music), played from 6pm to 11pm. (1-317 3596; www.karpatia.hu; V Ferenciek tere 7-8; mains 4300-8500Ft; 11am-11pm Mon-Fri, 5-11pm Sat & Sun; ; M M3 Ferenciek tere)

Baraka

FUSION **€€€**

7 MAP P82, B2

If you only eat in one fine-dining establishment while in Budapest, make it Baraka. You're ushered into the monochrome dining room, where chef André Bicalho works his magic in the half-open kitchen. Seafood features heavily, with French, Asian and Hungarian hints to the beautifully presented dishes. The bar, with its vast array of Japanese whiskies and pan-Asian tapas, is a treat. (1-200 0817; www.barakarestaurant.hu; V Dorottya utca 6; mains 7500-17,500Ft, 6-course tasting menus without/with wine pairing 27,900/41,900Ft; 6-11pm Mon-Sat; M M1 Vörösmarty tér)

Drinking

Good Spirit Bar

COCKTAIL BAR

8 MAP P82, D6

A welcoming watering hole, Good Spirit Bar comes fully stocked with more than 300 whiskies, with malts and blends from Scotland to Japan and even Hungary. Mixology lovers can take advantage of the bar's signature cocktails, featuring a few award-winning concoctions. (06 20 286 8040; https://goodspiritbar.hu; V Veres Pálné utca 7; 11am-midnight Mon-Sat; 15, 115, M M3 Ferenciek tere, 2)

Centrál Kávéház

CAFE

9 MAP P82, E5

This grande dame of a traditional cafe dates back to 1887. Awash with leather and dark wood inside, it's also a great spot for people-watching. It serves breakfast (2250Ft to 3250Ft) until 11.30am, as well as full meals and, of course, cakes and pastries (750Ft to 1450Ft). (1-266 2110, 06 30 382 3357; www.centralkavehaz.hu; V Károlyi utca 9; 8am-midnight; ; 15, 115, M M3 Ferenciek tere)

Entertainment

Akvárium Klub

LIVE MUSIC

10 MAP P82, D2

This place delivers a program of Hungarian and international live music, from indie, rock, world and pop to electronica and beyond. The main hall has capacity for 1500, a smaller hall fits 700 and a 'pub' holds 300. There are also regular club nights here, and a bar and bistro. A carpet of drinkers layers the terrace and steps in summer. (06 30 860 3368; www.akvariumklub.hu; V Erzsébet tér 12; noon-1am Sun-Tue, to 4.30am Wed-Sat; M M1/2/3 Deák Ferenc tér, 47, 49)

Shopping

Holló Műhely

ARTS & CRAFTS

11 MAP P82, E3

Off the northern end of Váci utca, this atelier-shop has attractive folk art with a modern look and remains a favourite place to shop for gifts. Lovely furniture and particularly beautiful painted Easter eggs. Find it on Facebook. (1- 317 8103; V Vitkovics Mihály utca 12; 10am-1pm & 1.30-6pm Mon-Fri, 10am-2pm Sat; M M1/2/3 Deák Ferenc tér, 47, 49)

Pannon Glove

CLOTHING

12 MAP P82, E4

This is an excellent place to buy high-quality fashion and winter leather gloves for both men and women. They are produced in the famous Bognár glove factory in Pécs in southern Hungary. Staff are knowledgeable and helpful. (1-483 0820, 06 30 940 7874; www.pannonpecsikesztyu.hu; V Károly körút 4; 10am-6pm Mon-Fri, to 3pm Sat; M M2 Astoria, 47, 49)

Vass Shoes

SHOES

13 MAP P82, C4

A traditional shoemaker that stocks ready-to-wear shoes and cobbles to order, Vass has a reputation that goes back to 1896; some people travel to Hungary just to have their footwear made here. (1-318 2375; www.vass-cipo.hu; V Haris köz 2; 10am-7pm Mon-Fri, to 3.30pm Sat; M M3 Ferenciek tere)

Magma

HOMEWARES

14 MAP P82, D4

This showroom in the heart of the Inner Town focuses on Hungarian design and designers exclusively, with everything from glassware, porcelain and toys to textiles and furniture. (1-235 0277; www.magma.hu; V Petőfi Sándor utca 11; 10am-7pm Mon-Fri, to 3pm Sat; M M3 Ferenciek tere)

Explore

Parliament & Around

To the north of Belváros is Lipótváros (Leopold Town), with the landmark Parliament facing the Danube to the west and the equally iconic Basilica of St Stephen to the east. This is prime sightseeing territory; here too are great galleries, some lovely squares and art nouveau buildings. East of Lipótváros lies Terézváros (Theresa Town), a district that gets very busy after dark.

The Short List

- ***Parliament (p90)*** *Entering the hallowed halls of Budapest's most iconic building.*
- ***Basilica of St Stephen (p92)*** *Visiting the final resting place of Hungary's most revered religious relic.*
- ***Royal Postal Savings Bank (p96)*** *Admiring the art nouveau building's sinuous curves and asymmetrical forms.*
- ***Szabadság tér (p96)*** *Wandering this beautiful square, one of Budapest's largest.*

Getting There & Around

V Szabadság tér for 15 to northern Pest; V Deák Ferenc tér for 16 to Castle Hill.

M M2 Kossuth Lajos tér, M3 Arany János utca and M1/2/3 Deák Ferenc tér.

Antall József rakpart for 2 to V Szent István körút; V Szent István körút for 4 or 6 to Buda or Big Ring Road in Pest.

Parliament & Around Map on p94

Parliament (p90)

Top Sight
Parliament

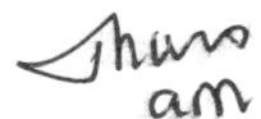

Hungary's Parliament stretches for 268m along the Danube in Pest from Kossuth Lajos tér. It's a vast, stately building and repository of national treasures that sits as a symbolic counterweight to the Royal Palace on Buda Hill on the opposite side of the river. Its strategic placement signifies that the nation's future lies with popular democracy and not royal prerogative.

MAP P94, A4

Országház

http://latogatokozpont.parlament.hu/en

V Kossuth Lajos tér 1-3

adult/student EU citizen 2400/1200Ft, non-EU citizen 6000/3100Ft

M M2 Kossuth Lajos tér, 2

Architecture

Designed by Imre Steindl in 1885, the building is a blend of many architectural styles (neo-Gothic, neo-Romanesque, neobaroque). Some 90 sculptures of the great and the good – kings, princes and historical figures – gaze out onto the Danube from the west facade, while the main door, the Lion Gate, gives on to revamped V Kossuth Lajos tér, which now contains a state-of-the-art visitors centre on its northern side.

Interior

You'll only get to see a handful of the 700 rooms here on a guided tour. From the visitors centre you ascend the 132 steps of the highly decorated Golden Staircase. Next is the centrepiece: the 16-sided, 66m-high Dome Hall where the Crown of St Stephen, the nation's most important national symbol, is on display, along with the 15th-century ceremonial sword, an orb (1301) and 10th-century Persian-made sceptre. The sweeping 96-step Grand Staircase (pictured) descends to the Lion Gate, but you'll move on to the 400-seat Congress Hall, where the upper house of the one-time bicameral assembly sat until 1944.

Crown of St Stephen

The two-part crown, with its characteristic bent cross, pendants hanging on either side and enamelled plaques of the Apostles on the band, dates from the late 12th century and has become the very symbol of the Hungarian nation. The crown has disappeared several times over the centuries – purloined or otherwise – only to reappear later. After WWII it was transferred to Fort Knox in Kentucky and not returned until 1978.

★ Top Tips

- You can join a 45-minute tour in any of eight languages; the English-language ones are usually at 10am, noon and then hourly on the half-hour 12.30pm to 4.30pm.
- Book ahead online through Jegymester (www.jegymester.hu)
- There are no tours while the National Assembly is in session.
- The ceremonial guards in the Dome Hall are on duty 24 hours; the guards at the flagpole outside change every hour between 8am and 7pm (earlier in winter).

✕ Take a Break

If you want to try authentic Hungarian sausage or salami, **Pick Deli & Gourmet** (☎1-331 7783; www.pickdeligourmet.hu; V Kossuth Lajos tér 9; mains 990-2390Ft; ⏰7am-5pm Mon-Fri), selling Hungary's most celebrated brand of prepared meat, is a revamped lunch spot and shop just opposite Parliament.

Top Sight

Basilica of St Stephen

The Basilica of St Stephen is the most sacred Catholic church in all of Hungary, if for no other reason than that it contains the nation's most revered relic: the mummified right hand of the church's patron, King St Stephen. It was built over half a century to 1905.

MAP P94, C7

Szent István Bazilika

www.basilica.hu

V Szent István tér

requested donation 200Ft

9am-7pm Mon-Sat, 7.45am-7pm Sun

M3 Arany János utca

The Dome

The facade of the basilica is anchored by two large towers, one of which contains a bell weighing 9.25 tonnes. Behind the towers is the 96m-high **dome** (Panoráma kilátó; 1-269 1849; www.basilica.hu; V Szent István tér; adult/child 600/400Ft; 10am-6pm Jun-Sep, to 5.30pm Apr, May & Oct, to 4.30pm Nov-Mar; M M3 Arany János utca), which can be reached by a lift and 42 steps (or 302 steps if you want to walk all the way). It offers one of the best views in the city.

The Interior

The basilica's interior is rather dark and gloomy, Károly Lotz's golden mosaics on the inside of the dome notwithstanding. Noteworthy items include Alajos Stróbl's statue of the king-saint on the main altar and Gyula Benczúr's painting of St Stephen dedicating Hungary to the Virgin Mary and Christ Child, to the right of the main altar.

The Holy Right Chapel

Behind the altar and to the left is the basilica's major drawcard: the Holy Right Chapel. It contains what is also known as the Holy Dexter, the mummified right hand of St Stephen and an object of great devotion. The chapel was being extensively renovated at the time of research and was not due to reopen before 2020.

The Treasury

As you enter the basilica there is a small lift to the right that will bring you to the 2nd-floor treasury of ecclesiastical objects, including censers, chalices, ciboria and vestments. Don't miss the art deco double monstrance (1938).

★ Top Tips

- Organ concerts (adult/student from 6000/5200Ft) are held here at 8pm, usually on Tuesday and Thursday throughout the year.
- English-language guided tours of the basilica (with/without dome visit 2000/1400Ft) usually depart at 10am and 3pm daily. Check the website to confirm.

Take a Break

Café Kör (1-311 0053; www.cafekor.net; V Sas utca 17; mains 1740-5890Ft; 10am-10pm Mon-Sat; 15, 115), just minutes away from the basilica, is a great place for lunch.

If you're looking for something fast and cheap for lunch, head round the corner for **Duran** (1-332 9348; www.duran.hu; V Október 6 utca 15; sandwiches 268-748Ft; 8am-5pm Mon-Fri, 9am-1pm Sat; 15) and some of their open-face sandwiches.

For reviews see

Top Sights	p90
Sights	p96
Eating	p97
Drinking	p99
Entertainment	p100
Shopping	p101

0 200 m
0 0.1 miles

A B C D E F
1 2 3 4

Szent István krt
Széchenyi rkp
Balassi Bálint u
BÁV
14
Moró Antik
Balaton u
Anna Antikvitás
Falk Miksa u
Honvéd u
Szemere u
Hegedűs Gyula u
Katona József u
ÚJLIPÓTVÁROS
Kresz Géza u
Visegrádi u
Kádár u
Váci út
Nyugati tér
Nyugati pu
Nyugati Train Station
Stollár Béla u
Honvéd tér
Nagy Ignác u
Bihari János u
Bajcsy-Zsilinszky út
Pintér Galéria
Markó u
Antall József rkp
Szalay u
Vajkay u
Parliament
Kossuth Lajos tér
Alkotmány u
LIPÓTVÁROS
Kozma F u
Kálmán Imre u
Vadász u
Báthory u
Nagymező u
Podmaniczky u
Weiner Leó u
Lovag u
Jókai u
Dessewffy u
Teréz krt
TERÉZVÁROS
Csengery u
Szondi u
Eötvös u

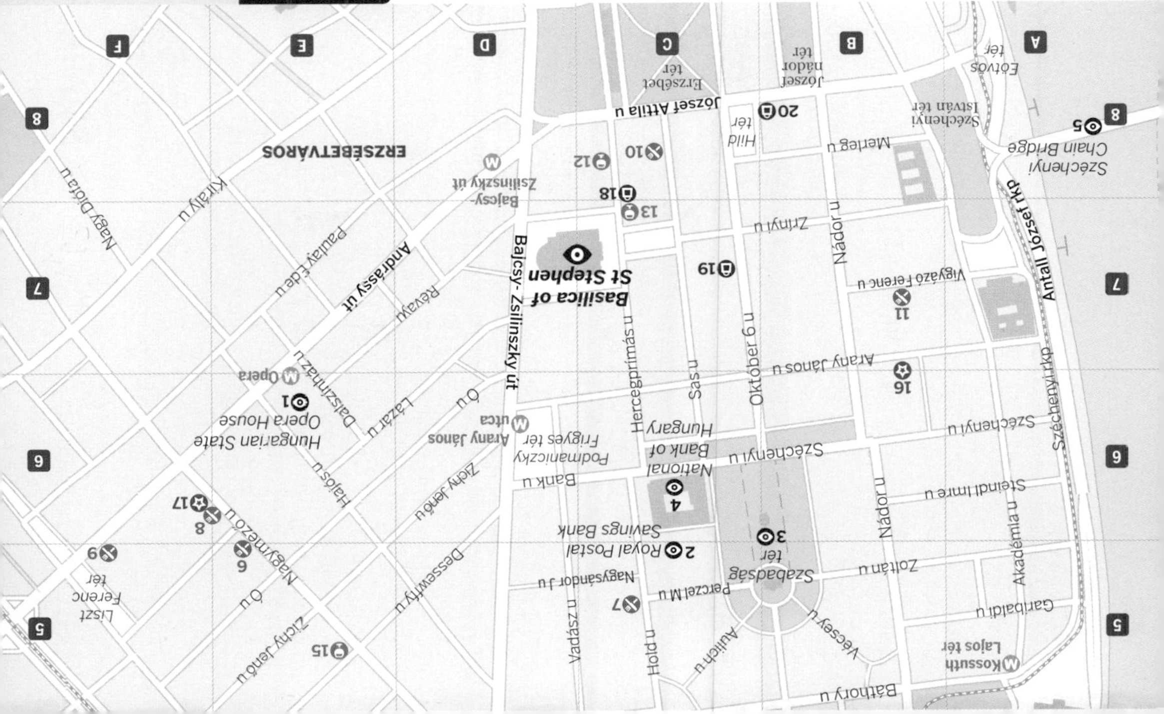

A B C D E F
5 6 7 8

ERZSÉBETVÁROS
Basilica of St Stephen
Hungarian State Opera House
1
Opera
2 Royal Postal Savings Bank
3 Szabadság tér
4 National Bank of Hungary
5 Széchenyi Chain Bridge
6
7
8
9
10
11
12
13
15
16
17
18
19
20
Kossuth Lajos tér
Arany János utca
Bajcsy-Zsilinszky út
Podmaniczky Frigyes tér
Liszt Ferenc tér
Erzsébet tér
József nádor tér
Széchenyi István tér
Eötvös tér
Hild tér
Andrássy út
Bajcsy-Zsilinszky út
Antall József rkp
Széchenyi rkp
Király u
Nagy Diófa u
Paulay Ede u
Révay u
Dalszínház u
Lázár u
Hajós u
Ó u
Zichy Jenő u
Nagymező u
Dessewffy u
Bank u
Vadász u
Hold u
Nagysándor J u
Perczel M u
Aulich u
Vécsey u
Báthory u
Zoltán u
Nádor u
Steindl Imre u
Széchenyi u
Akadémia u
Garibaldi u
Arany János u
Vigyázó Ferenc u
Merleg u
Zrínyi u
Október 6 u
Sas u
Hercegprímás u
József Attila u

Sights

Hungarian State Opera House

NOTABLE BUILDING

1 MAP P94, E6

The neo-Renaissance Hungarian State Opera House was designed by Miklós Ybl in 1884 and is among the most elegant buildings in Budapest. Its facade is decorated with statues of muses and opera greats such as Puccini, Mozart, Liszt and Verdi, while its interior dazzles with marble columns, gilded vaulted ceilings, chandeliers and near-perfect acoustics. If you cannot attend a performance, join one of the three 45-minute daily tours. Tickets are available from a desk in the lobby. (Magyar Állami Operaház; 06 30 279 5677, 1-332 8197; www.operavisit.hu; VI Andrássy út 22; adult/concession 2490/2200Ft; tours in English 2pm, 3pm & 4pm; M M1 Opera)

Royal Postal Savings Bank

NOTABLE BUILDING

2 MAP P94, C5

East of Szabadság tér, the former Royal Postal Savings Bank is a Secessionist extravaganza of colourful tiles and folk motifs, built by Ödön Lechner in 1901. One of the most beautiful buildings in Pest, it is now part of the National Bank of Hungary. (V Hold utca 4; 15)

Szabadság Tér

SQUARE

3 MAP P94, B6

This square, one of the largest in the city, is a few minutes' walk northeast of Széchenyi István tér. As you enter you'll pass a delightful **fountain** that works on optical sensors and turns off and on as you approach or back away from it, as well as the controversial **Antifascist Monument** (Antifasiszta emlékmű; V Szabadság tér; 15, 115, M M2 Kossuth Lajos tér) placed here in 2014. At the northern end is a **Soviet Army memorial** (Szovjet hadsereg emlékműve; V Szabadság tér; M M2 Kossuth Lajos tér), the last of its type still standing in the city. (Liberty Sq; 15, M M2 Kossuth Lajos tér)

National Bank of Hungary

NOTABLE BUILDING

4 MAP P94, C6

Southeast of Szabadság tér are some of the most striking buildings in Pest, including the National Bank of Hungary. It has terracotta reliefs on all four sides that illustrate trade and commerce through history: Arab camel traders, African rug merchants, Egyptian grain farmers, Chinese tea salesmen and the inevitable solicitor witnessing contracts. (Magyar Nemzeti Bank; V Szabadság tér 9; 15, 115)

Széchenyi Chain Bridge

BRIDGE

5 MAP P94, A8

Arguably the most striking of all the bridges in Budapest, twin-towered Széchenyi Chain Bridge, which is named in honour of its initiator, István Széchenyi, is particularly magical when it is lit up at night. The city's oldest span was actually built by Scotsman Adam Clark, who enjoys one of the few places that are reserved for foreigners in the Hungarian panoply of heroes. (Széchenyi lánchíd; 16, 105, 2, 19, 41)

Eating

Pizzica

PIZZA €

6 MAP P94, E5

If there is better pizza in Budapest, we don't know where to find it. Owned and operated by Italians Paolo and Enrico, Pizzica serves the real McCoy, with such toppings as potato and sage and mortadella. It's a tiny place but there's more seating in the small art gallery upstairs. (06 30 993 5481; www.facebook.com/pizzicapizza; VI Nagymező utca 21; pizza slices 290-490Ft, for 2 1690Ft; 11am-midnight Mon-Thu, to 3am Fri & Sat; M M1 Oktogon)

Széchenyi Chain Bridge

Kispiac

HUNGARIAN €€

This small retro-style restaurant – an absolute favourite of ours – serves seriously Hungarian things like stuffed *csülök* (pig's trotter – and way better than it sounds; 2950Ft), roast *malac* (piglet; 3250Ft) and the ever-popular wild boar spare ribs (3950Ft) as well as an infinite variety of *savanyúság* (pickled vegetables). Perfectly selected wine list and a warm welcome. (☎06 30 430 0142, 1-269 4231; www.kispiac.eu; V Hold utca 13; mains 2450-4450Ft; ⏲noon-10pm Mon-Sat; Ⓜ M3 Arany János utca)

Pesti Disznó Bisztró

HUNGARIAN €€

8 MAP P94, F6

Punters would be forgiven for thinking that the 'Pest Pig' was all about pork. In fact, of the 10 or so main courses more than half are beef, poultry, fish or vegetarian. It's a wonderful space, loft-like almost, with high tables and charming, informed service. The wine card is very, very good and most wines are available by the glass, too. (☎1-951 4061; www.pestidiszno.hu; VI Nagymező utca 19; mains 2790-6690Ft; ⏲9am-midnight; Ⓜ M1 Oktogon)

bigfish

SEAFOOD €€

9 MAP P94, F5

Select your fish or shellfish type from the ice trays, choose the cooking method and a side or two, and then sit back and wait for super-fresh seafood to be delivered to your table. This simply decorated restaurant has plenty of tables inside as well as on a terrace along Andrássy út. And there are bibs for you messy eaters, too. (☎06 30 527 2076, 1-269 0693; www.thebigfish.hu; VI Andrássy út 44; fish at market prices, sides 770-1200Ft, other mains 3600-4900Ft; ⏲noon-10pm; Ⓜ M1 Oktogon)

Borkonyha

HUNGARIAN €€€

10 MAP P94, C8

Chef Ákos Sárközi's approach to Hungarian cuisine at this Michelin-starred restaurant is contemporary, and the menu changes every week or two. Go for the signature foie gras appetiser with apple and celeriac and a glass of sweet Tokaji Aszú wine. If *mangalica* (a special type of Hungarian pork) is on the menu, try it with a glass of dry *furmint*. (Wine Kitchen; ☎1-266 0835; www.borkonyha.hu; V Sas utca 3; mains 3450-7950Ft; ⏲noon-4pm & 6pm-midnight Mon-Sat; 🚌15, 115, Ⓜ M1 Bajcsy-Zsilinszky út)

Mák Bisztró

INTERNATIONAL €€€

11 MAP P94, B7

The award-winning 'Poppy' offers inventive international dishes that lean in the direction of Hungary from a chalkboard menu that changes daily. Casual surrounds and seamless and very friendly service, with good advice on wine. At lunch the menu's two/three courses are a very budget-friendly

4200/4800Ft. (06 30 723 9383; www.mak.hu; V Vigyázó Ferenc utca 4; mains 5800-6800Ft; noon-3pm & 6pm-midnight Tue-Sat; 15, 115, 2)

Drinking

High Note Roof Bar ROOFTOP BAR

12 MAP P94, C8

If you need to impress someone – even yourself – lead them up to this rooftop bar above the **Aria Hotel** (1-445 4055; www.ariahotelbudapest.com; V Hercegprímás utca 5; d/ste from €220/640; P; 15,115, M M1 Bajcsy-Zsilinszky út). With your noses stuck into the dome of the basilica and virtually every landmark in Budapest within your grasp, you'll only be able to utter 'Wow!'. Great cocktails and friendly staff. What's not to love? Book ahead. (06 20 438 8648; www.highnoteskybar.hu/en; V Hercegprímás utca 5; noon-midnight; 15, 115, M M1 Bajcsy-Zsilinszky út)

DiVino Borbár WINE BAR

13 MAP P94, C7

Central and always heaving, DiVino is Budapest's most popular wine bar, as the crowds spilling out onto the square in front of the Basilica of St Stephen in the warm weather will attest. Choose from more than 120 wines produced by some three-dozen winemakers, but be careful: those 0.15dL (15mL) glasses (from 850Ft) go down quickly. Wine glass deposit is 500Ft. (06 70 935 3980; www.divinoborbar.hu; V Szent István tér 3; 4pm-midnight Sun-Wed, to 2am Thu-Sat; M M1 Bajcsy-Zsilinszky út)

Creamy salmon with spinach

Morrison's 2
CLUB

14 MAP P94, C1

Far and away Budapest's biggest party venue, this cavernous club attracts a younger crowd with its six dance floors and as many bars (including one in a covered courtyard and one with table football). Great DJs. The cover charge is 500Ft. (1-374 3329; www.morrisons2.hu; V Szent István körút 11; 5pm-6am; 4, 6)

Alterego
GAY

15 MAP P94, E5

Still Budapest's premier gay club, Alterego has the chicest crowd and the best dance music on offer. Don't miss the drag shows by Lady Dömper and the Alterego Trans Company. Always a hoot. (06 70 345 4302, 06 70 565 1111; www.alteregoclub.hu; VI Dessewffy utca 33; 10pm-5am Fri, to 6am Sat; 4, 6)

Garden Clubs & Ruin Bars

A visit to Budapest during summer is not complete without an evening in one of the city's many so-called *kertek*, literally 'gardens' but in Budapest any outdoor spot that has been converted into an entertainment zone. These often rough-and-ready venues, including courtyards, rooftops and *romkocsmák* (ruin pubs) that rise phoenix-like from abandoned buildings, can change from year to year and are seasonal, but some of the more successful ones, like **Szimpla Kert** (p125), are now permanent and open year-round.

Entertainment

Aranytíz House of Culture
TRADITIONAL MUSIC

At this cultural centre in Lipótváros, there are wonderful mixed traditional *táncház* (folk music and dance) from 8pm on Saturday that run till about midnight. Bring the kids in earlier (about 6pm) for the children's version. Check the website for programs. (Aranytíz Kultúrház; 1-354 3400; www.aranytiz.hu; V Arany János utca 10; adult/child 1000/500Ft; box office 2-9pm Mon & Wed, 9am-3pm Sat; 15, 115, 2)

Budapest Operetta
OPERA

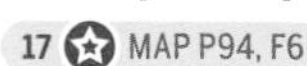

This theatre presents operettas, which are always a riot, especially campy ones like *The Gypsy Princess* by Imre Kálmán or Ferenc Lehár's *The Merry Widow*, with their over-the-top staging and costumes. Think baroque Gilbert and Sullivan – and then some. There's an interesting bronze statue of Kálmán outside the main entrance. (Budapesti Operettszínház; 1-472 2030, box office 1-312 4866; www.operettszinhaz.hu; VI Nagymező utca 17; tickets 1000-13,500Ft; box office 10am-7pm Mon-Fri, 1-7pm Sat & Sun; trolleybus 70, 78, M1 Opera)

Antiques Browsing

One of our favourite places to while away part or all of a Saturday morning is along V Falk Miksa utca, which is lined with antique and curio shops. Start at the northern end with **BÁV** (Bizományi Kereskedőház és Záloghitel; Map p94, B1; ☎06 20 777 2583, 1-473 0666; www.bav.hu/en/store/szent-istvan-antik; XIII Szent István körút 3; ⏰10am-6pm Mon-Fri, to 2pm Sat; 🚊2, 4, 6) to get an idea of what your average householder might be getting rid of during spring cleaning, then move south on to the various other shops like **Moró Antik** (Map p94, B2; ☎1-311 0814; www.moroantik.hu; V Falk Miksa utca 13; ⏰10am-6pm Mon-Fri, to 1pm Sat; 🚊2, 4, 6) and **Anna Antikvitás** (Map p94, B2; ☎06 20 935 0374, 1-302 5461; www.annaantikvitas.eu; V Falk Miksa utca 18-20; ⏰10am-6pm Mon-Fri, to 1pm Sat; 🚊2, 4, 6), ending up at the largest of them all: **Pintér Galéria** (Map p94, B3; ☎06 30 331 0600, 1-311 3030; www.pinteraukcioshaz.hu; V Falk Miksa utca 10; ⏰10am-6pm Mon-Fri, to 2pm Sat; 🚊2, 4, 6).

Shopping

Memories of Hungary — ARTS & CRAFTS

18 MAP P94, C8

One of our favourite places to buy souvenirs and gifts, this shop has (mostly genuine) Hungarian handicrafts as well as a good selection of local foodstuffs and wine. It's also useful as an information point. (☎06 30 732 6511, 1-780 5844; www.memoriesofhungary.hu; V Hercegprímás utca 8; ⏰10am-10pm; 🚌15, 115, Ⓜ M1 Bajcsy-Zsilinszky út, M3 Arany János utca)

Bestsellers — BOOKS

19 MAP P94, C7

Still top of the pops for English-language bookshops in Budapest, with fiction, travel guides and lots of Hungarica, as well as a large selection of newspapers and magazines overseen by master bookseller Tony Láng. Helpful staff are at hand to advise and recommend. (☎1-312 1295; www.bestsellers.hu; V Október 6 utca 11; ⏰9am-6.30pm Mon-Fri, 11am-6pm Sat, noon-6pm Sun; 🚌15, 115, Ⓜ M1/2/3 Deák Ferenc tér)

Malatinszky Wine Store — WINE

20 MAP P94, B8

Owned and operated by a one-time sommelier at the Gundel restaurant, this shop has an excellent selection of high-end Hungarian wines, including three vintages from his own organically farmed vines. Ask the staff to recommend a bottle. (☎1-317 5919; www.malatinszky.hu; V József Attila utca 12; ⏰10am-1pm & 1.30-6pm Mon-Sat; 🚌16, 105, Ⓜ M1/2/3 Deák Ferenc tér, 🚊2)

MARGI ZIGETI SZABADTER SZÍNPAD
MARGIT
TERASZ • TERRACE
ÉTTEREM • RESTAURANT

Explore

Margaret Island & Northern Pest

Neither Buda nor Pest, leafy, 2.5km-long Margaret Island (Margit-sziget) lies in the middle of the Danube. The island is not overly endowed with important sights, but you can easily spend half a day exploring its swimming complexes, thermal spa, gardens and centuries-old ruins. To the east, Újlipótváros (New Leopold Town) has tree-lined streets and is perfect for lunch or coffee.

The Short List

- ***Palatinus Strand (p105)*** *Splashing and soaking year-round (finally) at Budapest's best swimming pool complex.*
- ***Dominican Convent (p105)*** *Revisiting Budapest's medieval past at these ruins on Margaret Island.*
- ***Pinball Museum (p106)*** *Imitating Elton John in the film Tommy and playing on any of the 140 vintage pinball machines.*

Getting There & Around

Tram: Both districts served by trams 4 and 6. Tram 2 to XIII Jászai Mari tér from the Belváros.

Bus: 26 covers the length of Margaret Island running between Nyugati train station and Árpád Bridge. Újlipótváros can be reached via bus 15 and 115.

Trolleybus: 75 and 76 are excellent for Újlipótváros.

M The eastern end of Újlipótváros is best reached by metro (M3 Nyugati pályaudvar).

Margaret Island & Northern Pest Map on p104

Water tower and open-air theatre (p106)

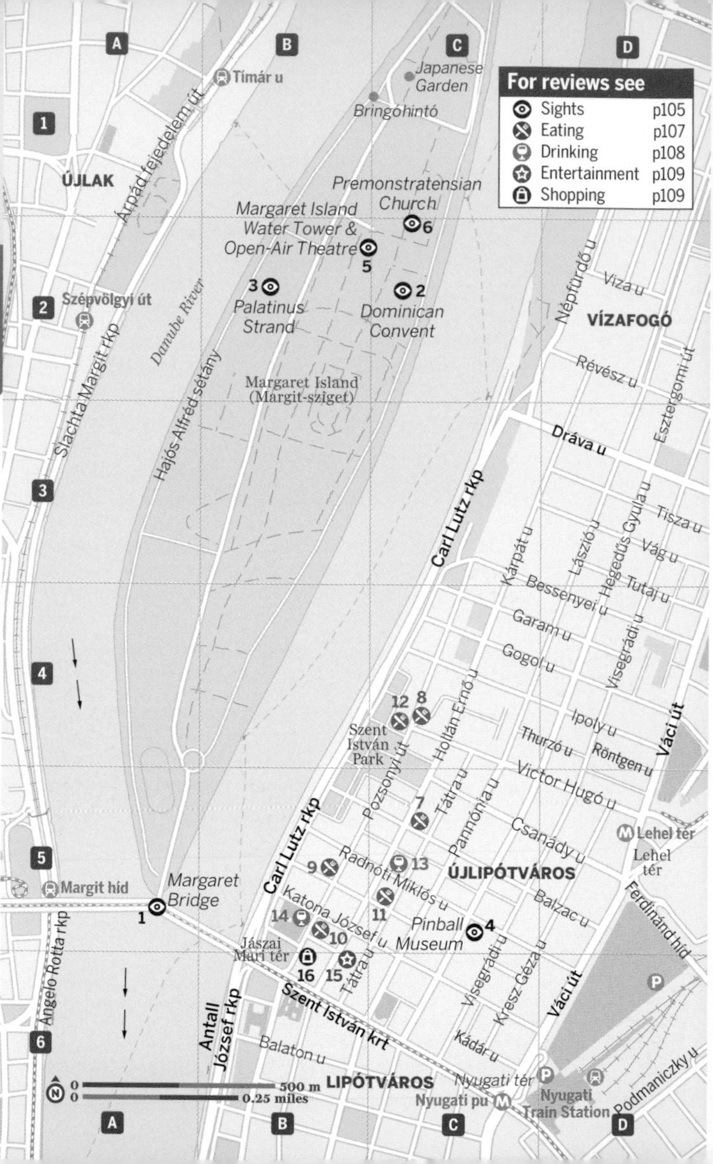
For reviews see
Sights p105
Eating p107
Drinking p108
Entertainment p109
Shopping p109
A
B
C
D
1
2
3
4
5
6
Tímár u
Japanese Garden
Bringóhintó
ÚJLAK
Árpád fejedelem út
Premonstratensian Church
6
Margaret Island Water Tower & Open-Air Theatre
5
3
Palatinus Strand
2
Dominican Convent
Szépvölgyi út
Danube River
Népfürdő u
Viza u
VÍZAFOGÓ
Révész u
Esztergomi út
Slachta Margit rkp
Hajós Alfréd sétány
Margaret Island (Margit-sziget)
Dráva u
Carl Lutz rkp
Tisza u
Kárpát u
László u
Hegedűs Gyula u
Vág u
Tutaj u
Bessenyei u
Garam u
Gogol u
Visegrádi u
12
8
Szent István Park
Hollán Ernő u
Ipoly u
Thurzó u
Röntgen u
Váci út
Victor Hugó u
Pozsonyi út
Tátra u
7
Pannónia u
Csanády u
Lehel tér
Carl Lutz rkp
9
Radnóti Miklós u
13
ÚJLIPÓTVÁROS
Balzac u
Ferdinánd híd
Margit híd
Margaret Bridge
1
14
Katona József u
11
10
Pinball Museum
4
Jászai Mari tér
16
15
Tátra u
Visegrádi u
Kresz Géza u
Váci út
Angelo Rotta rkp
Antall József rkp
Szent István krt
Kádár u
Balaton u
LIPÓTVÁROS
Nyugati tér
Podmaniczky u
Nyugati pu
Nyugati Train Station
0 500 m
0 0.25 miles

Sights

Margaret Bridge

BRIDGE

1 MAP P104, A5

Renovated Margaret Bridge introduces the Big Ring Road to Buda. It's unique in that it doglegs in order to stand at right angles to the Danube where it converges at the southern tip of Margaret Island. The bridge was originally built by French engineer Ernest Goüin in 1876; the spur leading to the island was added in 1901. (Margit-híd; 26, 226, 2, 4, 6)

Dominican Convent

RUINS

2 MAP P104, C2

A ruin is all that remains of the 13th-century convent built by Béla IV where his daughter St Margaret (1242–71) took the veil. A red marble sepulchre cover surrounded by an iron grille marks her original resting place and there's a lookout over the ruins. (Domonkos kolostor; XIII Margit-sziget; 26, 226)

Palatinus Strand

SWIMMING

3 MAP P104, B2

Now open year-round with the addition of four covered pools, 'Palatinus Beach', the largest swimming complex in the capital, counts some 10 pools (two with thermal water), wave machines, water slides and kids pools. (1-340 4500; www.palatinusstrand.hu; XIII Margit-sziget; adult/child May-Sep Mon-Fri 3100/2400Ft, Sat & Sun 3500/2600Ft, Oct-Apr Mon-Fri 2400/2000Ft, Sat & Sun 2800/2300Ft; 8am-8pm; 26)

Palatinus Strand

St Margaret

The island's most famous resident – and namesake – was Béla IV's daughter Margaret (1242–71). The king supposedly pledged her to a life of devotion in a nunnery if the Mongols, who had overrun Hungary in 1241–42, were expelled. They were and she was – at age nine. Still, she seemed to enjoy it (if we're to believe *The Lives of the Saints*), especially the mortification-of-the-flesh parts. Canonised only in 1943, St Margaret commands something of a cult following in Hungary.

Pinball Museum

MUSEUM

4 MAP P104, C5

This quirky museum that is housed in a basement is one of Budapest's hidden attractions. It's home to 140 vintage pinball museums – yes, you can play all but the oldest wooden models dating back as far as 1947. As the largest such collection in Europe that's not only accessible to the public but also interactive, it has quite a cult following and is always busy. (Flippermúzeum; 06 30 900 6091; www.flippermuzeum.hu; XIII Radnóti Miklós utca 18; adult/under 26yr 3000/2000Ft; 4pm-midnight Wed-Fri, 2pm-midnight Sat, 10am-10pm Sun; 15, 115, trolleybus 75, 76)

Water Tower & Open-Air Theatre

ARCHITECTURE

5 MAP P104, B2

Erected in 1911 in the north-central part of Margaret Island, the octagonal water tower rises 57m above the **open-air theatre** *(szabadtéri színpad)* to the south, which is used for concerts and plays in summer. The tower contains the **Lookout Gallery** (Kilátó Galéria) reached by climbing 152 steps. The 360-degree view of the island is pleasant but consists mostly of treetops. (Margitszigeti Víztorony és Szabadtéri Színpad; 1-301 0147, 1-340 4196; www.szabadter.hu; XIII Margit-sziget; Lookout Gallery adult/concession 600/300Ft; Lookout Gallery 11am-7pm Jun-Sep; 26, 226)

Premonstratensian Church

CHURCH

6 MAP P104, C2

This Romanesque Premonstratensian Church, dedicated to St Michael by the order of White Canons and reconstructed in 1931, dates back originally to the 12th century. Its 15th-century bell mysteriously appeared one night in 1914 under the roots of a walnut tree knocked over in a storm. It was probably buried by monks during the Turkish invasion. (Premontre templom; XIII Margit-sziget; 26, 226)

Eating

Oriental Soup House

VIETNAMESE €

7 MAP P104, C5

Though it's situated far away from central Budapest, this authentic Vietnamese joint is regularly packed. Customers squeeze around the communal tables that are arranged beneath paper lanterns and tuck into several kinds of *pho* (rice noodle soup), as well as *mien ga* (chicken noodle soup) and *bun cha* (grilled pork and noodles). (☎06 70 617 3535; www.facebook.com/orientalsouphouse; XIII Hollán Ernő utca 35; mains 1290-1990Ft; 🕐11.30am-10pm; ✎; 🚌trolleybus 75, 76, 🚌15, 115)

Sarki Fűszeres

CAFE €

8 MAP P104, C4

This delightful retro-style cafe located on tree-lined Pozsonyi út is the perfect place to grab brunch, a late breakfast, a speciality coffee or just a quick sandwich. It also doubles as a deli/wine shop. (Corner Grocery Store; ☎1-238 0600; www.facebook.com/sarkifuszeres; XIII Pozsonyi út 53-55; breakfast 950-1650Ft, sandwiches 1750-2550Ft; 🕐8am-9pm Mon-Thu, to 10pm Fri & Sat, 9am-5pm Sun; 🚌trolleybus 75, 76, 🚌15, 115)

Édesmindegy

CAFE €

9 MAP P104, B5

Come to this *desszertbár* for some of Budapest's best and most imaginative cakes. Temptations include cherry cheesecake with Sichuan pepper, chocolate tart with salted caramel and probably the best *pasteis de nata* (custard tarts) outside Lisbon. (☎06 30 502 9358; www.facebook.com/Edesmindegy; XIII Pozsonyi út 16; cakes 840-960Ft; 🕐9am-9pm; 🚌trolleybus 75, 76, 🚋4, 6)

Babka

MEDITERRANEAN €€

10 MAP P104, B5

Babka has fast become the go-to dining option in Újlipótváros for its excellent dishes, friendly service and hip crowd. It calls itself 'Mediterranean', but the large choice of mezze-style dishes and the eponymous cake from Jerusalem (600Ft) made with chocolate, walnuts and orange put it further east on our map. The small plate mezze

Cycle the Island

Margaret Island is bigger than you think, so rent a bicycle or other wheeled conveyance from **Bringóhintó** (Map p104, C1; ☎1-329 2073; www.bringohinto.hu; XIII Margit-sziget; per 30min/60min/day mountain bikes 720/990/2800Ft, pedal coaches for 4 people 2680/3980Ft; 🕐8am-dusk; 🚌26, 226), at the refreshment stand near the **Japanese Garden** (Japánkert; Map p104, C1; XIII Margit-sziget; 🚌26, 226) in the northern part of the island.

Bunny Years

Margaret Island was always the domain of one religious order or another until the Turks came along and turned what was then called the Island of Rabbits into – appropriately enough – a harem, from which all 'infidels' were barred. It's been a public park open to everyone since the mid-19th century, though you may encounter some harem-like activity if you stray too far off the path in the twilight.

combo (3000Ft) is great value. (1-789 9672; https://babkabudapest.business.site; XIII Pozsonyi út 3; mains 2400-6900Ft; 8am-midnight Sun-Wed, to 1am Thu-Sat; trolleybus 75, 76, 4, 6)

Firkász

HUNGARIAN €€

Originally set up by former journalists, retro-style restaurant 'Hack' has been one of our favourite Hungarian 'nostalgia' eateries for years, thanks to the lovely old mementoes on the walls, great homestyle dishes such as roast goose leg in red wine (3990Ft) and Carpathian-style pike-perch (4490Ft), a good wine list and nightly live music from 7pm. (06 70 432 8050, 1-450 1118; www.firkasz.hu; XIII Tátra utca 18; mains 3500-7990Ft; noon-11pm; 15, 115, 4, 6)

Dunapark

CAFE €€

12 MAP P104, C4

Built in 1938 as a cinema, this art deco place with a lovely upstairs gallery, outdoor terrace and views of Szent István Park is a fine restaurant serving an excellent pork ragout that is made with dark beer (3590Ft) and salmon ravioli (3990Ft). But we often use it as a *cukrászda* (cake shop) as its cakes (490Ft to 990Ft) are sublime. (1-786 1009; www.dunaparkkavehaz.com; XIII Pozsonyi út 38 & Szent István Park 27; mains 2990-5990Ft; 8am-11pm Mon-Fri, 10am-11pm Sat, to 10pm Sun; trolleybus 75, 76, 15, 115)

Drinking

Raj Ráchel Tortaszalon

CAFE

13 MAP P104, C5

What is probably the first kosher cake shop–cafe to open in Újlipótváros since WWII serves all the usual favourites, including the city's best – trust us – *flódni* (a three-layer cake; 900Ft), which is usually a three-layer cake with apple, walnut and poppy-seed fillings but Ráchel adds her grandma's plum jam. (Ráchel Raj Cake Shop; 1-787 6088, 06 20 492 7062; http://raj-rachel-blog.torta.hu; XIII Hollán Ernő utca 25; 11am-7pm Mon-Fri, 10am-7pm Sat & Sun; trolleybus 75, 76, 15, 115)

LA Bodegita

COCKTAIL BAR

14 MAP P104, B5

The Caribbean-style food here is missable, but you should definitely taste master mixologist András Lajsz's incomparable American-style (hi, LA!) cocktails; he does a mean Cosmo and we also like his Bodeguita Colada. Moody piano music some nights, Cuban at the weekend. (06 20 945 6156, 1-789 4019; www.labodegita.hu; XIII Pozsonyi út 4; cocktails 1400-1900Ft; 11am-midnight Mon-Wed, to 2am Thu-Sat, to 10pm Sun; trolleybus 75, 76, 2, 4, 6)

Entertainment

Budapest Jazz Club

JAZZ

15 MAP P104, B6

A very sophisticated venue – now pretty much the most serious one in town – for traditional, vocal and Latin jazz by local and international talent. Past international performers have included Terrence Blanchard, the Yellowjackets and Liane Carroll. Concerts most nights at 8pm or 8.30pm, with jam sessions at 10pm or 11pm on Friday, Saturday and Monday. (1-798 7289; www.bjc.hu; XIII Hollán Ernő utca 7; 10am-midnight Sun-Thu, to 2am Fri & Sat, varies Sun; trolleybus 75, 76, 15, 115)

Steak with baked potatoes at Firkász

Shopping

Mézes Kuckó

FOOD

16 MAP P104, B6

This small shop is the place to go if you have the urge for something sweet; its nut-and-honey cookies (280Ft per 100g) are to die for. A decorated heart-shaped *mézeskalács* (honey cake) makes a lovely gift. Four different types of honey available too. (Honey Nook; 06 20 344 5778; www.facebook.com/pages/category/Grocery-Store/Mézes-Kuckó-Bt-382532878777794/; XIII Jászai Mari tér 4; 10am-6pm Mon-Fri, 9am-1pm Sat; 2, 4, 6)

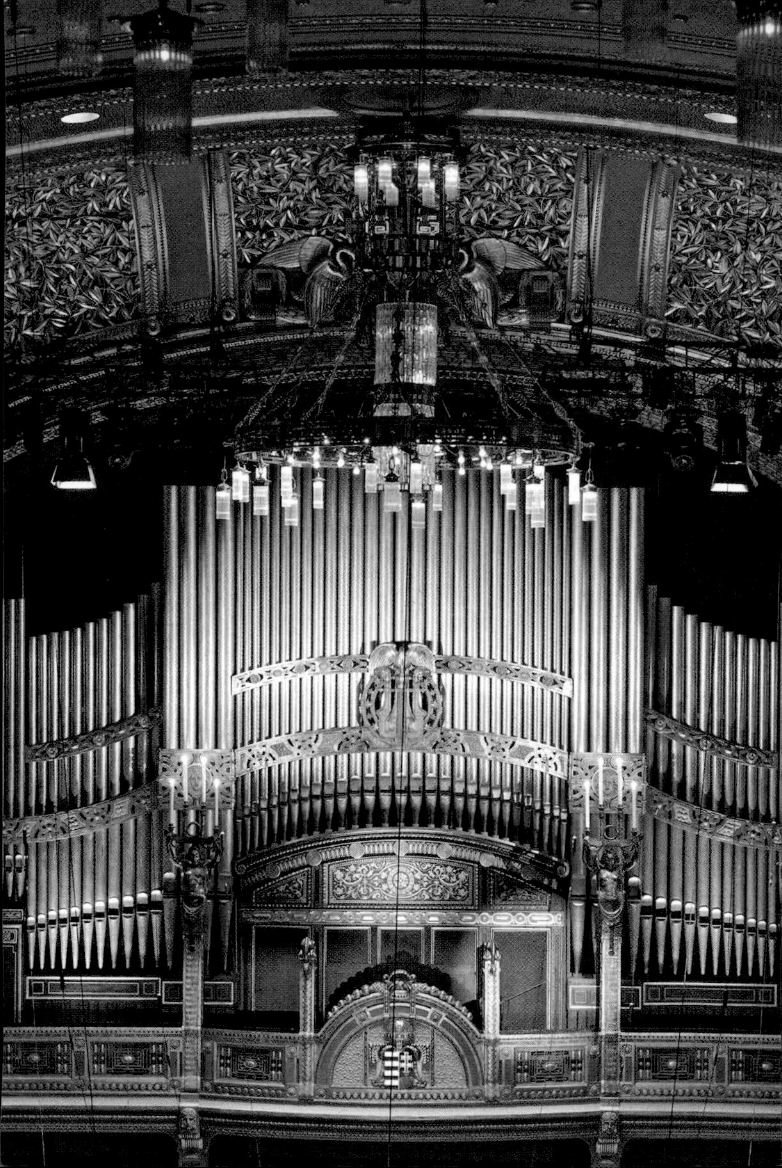

Explore Erzsébetváros & the Jewish Quarter

This neighbourhood takes in Erzsébetváros (Elizabeth Town) and most of Terézváros, including well- and high-heeled Andrássy út, the long, dramatic and very chic boulevard that slices through Terézváros. It hosts a large percentage of Budapest's accommodation at all levels, restaurants serving everything from Chinese and Indian vegetarian to French and Serbian, and the city's hottest nightspots.

The Short List

- ***Great Synagogue (p112)*** *Marvelling at the exotic architecture of what is the largest Jewish house of worship in Europe.*
- ***Liszt Music Academy (p120)*** *Attending a concert at the city's most important (and beautiful) classical-music venue.*
- ***Andrássy út (p120)*** *Strolling along this gracious tree-, shop- and sight-lined boulevard, listed as a Unesco World Heritage Site.*

Getting There & Around

M M1/2/3 Deák Ferenc tér, M1 Oktogon, M2/4 Blaha Lujza tér and Keleti pályaudvar, M2 Astoria.

VII Erzsébet körút for 4 or 6 to Buda or the rest of Pest's Big Ring Road; 47 and 49 are for western Erzsébetváros.

VII Wesselényi utca and Dohány utca for 74 to the Little Ring Road or City Park.

Erzsébetváros & the Jewish Quarter Map on p118

Pipe organ at Liszt Music Academy (p120) POSZTOS / SHUTTERSTOCK ©

Top Sight

Great Synagogue

Budapest's Great Synagogue, with its red-and-yellow brick facade and two enormous Moorish-style towers, is the largest Jewish house of worship in the world outside New York City, seating 3000 worshippers. Built in 1859, the Neolog (or Conservative – not Orthodox) synagogue contains both Romantic-style and Moorish architectural elements. It is also called Dohány utca Synagogue (Dohány utcai Zsinagóga).

MAP P118, B8

Nagy Zsinagóga

www.greatsynagogue.hu/gallery_syn.html

VII Dohány utca 2

adult/concession/family incl museum 4000/3000/9000Ft

M M2 Astoria, 47, 49

Rose Window

Because some elements of the synagogue recall Christian churches – including the central rose window with an inscription from the second book of Moses – the synagogue is sometimes called the 'Jewish cathedral'. It was renovated in the 1990s thanks to private donations, including US$5 million from the American cosmetic magnate Estée Lauder (1908–2004), born in New York to Hungarian Jewish immigrants.

Interior Fittings

Don't miss the decorative carvings on the Ark of the Covenant by National Romantic architect Frigyes Feszl, who also did the wall and ceiling frescoes of multicoloured and gold geometric shapes. Both Franz Liszt and Camille Saint-Saëns played on the rebuilt 5000-pipe organ dating back to 1859.

Jewish Museum & Archives

The **Hungarian Jewish Museum & Archives** (Magyar Zsidó Múzeum és Levéltár; www.milev.hu), upstairs in an annexe of the synagogue, contains objects related to religious and everyday life. Interesting items include 3rd-century Jewish headstones from Roman Pannonia discovered in 1792 in Nagykanizsa in southwestern Hungary, a vast amount of liturgical items in silver, and manuscripts, including a handwritten book of the local Burial Society from the late 18th century.

Holocaust Tree of Life Memorial

In Raoul Wallenberg Memorial Park on the synagogue's north side and opposite VII Wesselényi utca 6, the Holocaust Tree of Life Memorial, designed by Imre Varga in 1991, stands over the mass graves of those murdered by the Nazis in 1944–45. On the leaves of the metal 'tree of life' are the family names of some of the hundreds of thousands of victims.

★ Top Tips

- A two-hour **Jewish Heritage Tours** (1-317 1377; www.ticket.info.hu; V Zrínyi utca 5, Duna Palota; M M1/2/3 Deák Ferenc tér, 47, 49) walk (adult/student 7400/7000Ft) of the Jewish Quarter departs from the Great Synagogue at 10am Sunday to Friday and at 2pm Monday to Thursday March to October.
- A plaque on the Great Synagogue notes that Tivadar (Theodore) Herzl, the father of modern Zionism, was born on the site in 1860.
- Get one of the free audio guides available in a dozen languages; labelling in the Hungarian Jewish Museum is poor.

Take a Break

Have a bite at Kőleves (p124) which, though not kosher, serves Jewish specialities. For something sweet – and kosher – head for Fröhlich Cukrászda (p122). Its *flódni* (a three-layer cake) is legendary.

Walking Tour

Historic Jewish Quarter

This section of Erzsébetváros, stretching between the Big and Little Ring Rds, has always been predominantly Jewish, and this was the ghetto where Jews were forced to live behind wooden fences when the Nazis occupied Hungary in 1944. Walking through its streets is like stepping back in time.

Walk Facts

Start VI Liszt Ferenc tér

End VII Dohány utca

Length 1km; one to two hours

❶ Liszt Music Academy

Begin the walk in restaurant- and cafe-packed VI Liszt Ferenc tér, and poke your head into the sumptuous **Liszt Music Academy** (p120). Promise yourself you'll attend a concert.

❷ Church of St Teresa

Walking southwest along Király utca you'll pass the **Church of St Teresa**, built in 1811 and containing a massive neoclassical altar designed by Mihály Pollack in 1822. At Király utca 47 (and directly opposite the church) is an interesting neo-Gothic house built in 1847, with a delightful oriel window.

❸ Klauzál Tér

Turning into Csányi utca, head southeast over Dob utca to the heart of the old Jewish Quarter, Klauzál tér. The square still has a feeling of prewar Budapest. A continued Jewish presence is evident in the surrounding streets – with several kosher restaurants, a kosher butcher just next to the **Orthodox Synagogue** (p121) and the wonderful **Fröhlich Cukrászda** (p122) cake shop.

❹ Ghetto Memorial

Walk up Holló utca and turn left. If the gate at Király utca 15 is open, walk to the courtyard's rear to see a 30m-long stretch of the original **ghetto wall**, rebuilt in 2010. Otherwise, just peer through the slit in the gate. Votive lamps and stones stand before it in tribute to victims of the Holocaust.

❺ Gozsdu Udvar

The next turning on the left is the passageway called **Gozsdu udvar** (1901); now the district's number-one nightlife destination, it's lined with bars, cafes and restaurants, and pulses with music and merry-makers in the evening.

❻ Monuments & Murals

At Dob utca 12 is an unusual anti-fascist **monument to Carl Lutz**, a Swiss consul who, like Raoul Wallenberg, provided Jews with false papers in 1944. It portrays an angel on high sending down a long bolt of cloth to a victim.

❼ Street Art

Just around the corner, bordering a car park, are two large **murals**. The one on the left (2013) commemorates the 60th anniversary of the football victory of Hungary's 'Golden Team', the first time a continental team beat England at Wembley (6–3). The one on the right is an oversized Rubik's Cube, the frustratingly difficult 3D puzzle invented in 1974 by Hungarian sculptor and architecture professor Ernő Rubik.

❽ Great Synagogue

Retrace your steps and you'll find the **Great Synagogue** (p112) at the end of the street.

Walking Tour

Bar-Hopping in Erzsébetváros

Wander along Király utca or down Gozsdu udvar on a Friday night and it can feel like the whole world and their best friends are here. And jostling with wide-eyed tourists and hen and stag parties may leave you wondering whether the locals have deserted this area altogether. They haven't – you just need to know where to find them.

Getting There

M M1 Oktogon, M1/2/3 Deák Ferenc tér

4, 6, 47, 49

70, 78

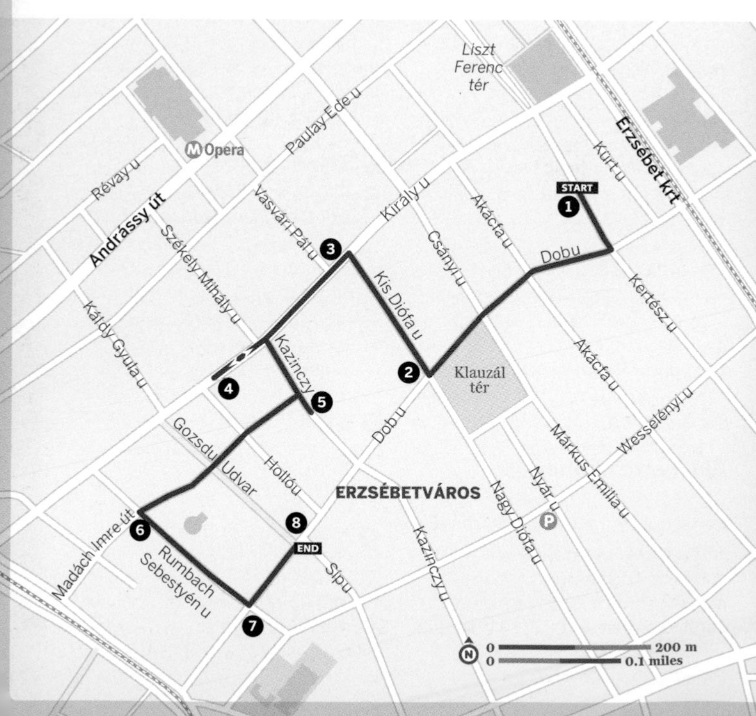

❶ Try Hungarian Craft Beer

Tiny **Csak a Jó Sör** (www.csakajosor.hu; VII Kertész utca 42-44; ⌚2-9pm Mon-Sat; M M1 Oktogon, 🚊4, 6) closes early, so it's a good place to start your evening. True to the name, which translates as 'only good beer', the shelves of this tiny shop are stacked high with brown bottles containing an extensive selection of international bottled craft beer.

❷ Check Out a Tiny Local Bar

With your appetite whetted, it's just a short hop to **Kisüzem** (www.facebook.com/Kisuzem; VII Kis Diófa utca 2; ⌚noon-2am Sun-Wed, to 3am Thu-Sat; 📶; 🚌trolleybus 70, 78, 🚊4, 6), where relaxed drinkers hang out on the bar's little outside benches. Head inside for another beer or *pálinka* (fruit brandy) and to check out what live jazz, folk and experimental music is on.

❸ Taste Hungarian Wine

On bustling Király utca, **Kadarka** (www.facebook.com/kadarkabar; VII Király utca 42; ⌚4pm-midnight; 📶; M M1 Opera) offers a huge list of Hungarian wines in a modern, sociable bar. Take a table on the street for a spot of people-watching or settle on a tall bar stool inside.

❹ Try a Tiki Tacky Cocktail

Just a block to the west is the **Rumpus Tiki Bar** (http://rumpus.hu; VII Király utca 19; ⌚6pm-2am Sun-Wed, to 4am Thu-Sat; 🚌trolleybus 70, 78, M M1/2/3 Deák Ferenc tér), and who isn't a sucker for a tiki bar, with those fake coconut trees, palm-frond huts, colourful idols, and mai tais and piña coladas?

❺ Visit a Garden Club

At **Mika Tivadar Mulató** (www.mikativadarmulato.hu; VII Kazinczy utca 47; ⌚4pm-midnight Mon-Wed, to 4am Thu, to 5am Fri & Sat; M M1/2/3 Deák Ferenc tér) a short walk southeast you'll find a ground-floor bar, a venue downstairs and a garden courtyard, which is one of the best *romkertek* (ruin gardens) in town.

❻ Stroll Bar-Lined Streets

Just down the road, Madách Imre út is usually packed. Many bars line the pedestrian alley, but locals favour **Központ** (www.facebook.com/kozpontbudapest; VII Madách Imre út 5; ⌚8am-1am Mon-Wed, to 2am Thu, to 3am Fri & Sat, noon-10pm Sun; M M1/2/3 Deák Ferenc tér).

❼ Mezze at Dobrumba

If you're feeling peckish head south down Rumbach Sebestyén utca to **Dobrumba** (p123) for some of the best mezze in town.

❽ Head for a Salsa Party

If you're ready to ramp things up a bit, head back towards Gozsdu udvar, where the bar-restaurant **Vicky Barcelona** (www.facebook.com/vickybarcelonatapas; VII Gozsdu udvar, VII Dob utca 16; ⌚5pm-3am Mon-Wed, to 4am Thu, to 5am Fri & Sat, noon-4am Sun; M M2 Astoria) transforms into one big salsa music and dance party after 11pm.

For reviews see
Top Sights p112
Sights p120
Eating p122
Drinking p125
Entertainment p126
Shopping p127
0 200 m
0 0.1 miles
A
B
C
D
E
F
1
2
3
4
WESTEND CITY CENTER
Nyugati Train Station
Nyugati tér
Nyugati pu
Váci út
Kresz Géza u
Ferdinánd híd
Podmaniczky u
Székely Bertalan u
Szinyei Merse u
Bajnok u
Kmetty György u
Szív u
Rózsa u
Izabella u
Szondi u
Aradi u
Kodály körönd
Benczúr u
Bajza u
Felső erdősor
Andrássy út
Rottenbiller u
Városligeti fasor
Lövölde tér
TERÉZVÁROS
26
Vörösmarty u
Szobi u
Jókai u
Teréz krt
Eötvös u
Csengery u
Bajcsy-Zsilinszky út
Weiner Leó u
Lovag u
Dessewffy u
Zichy Jenő u
Nagymező u
Hajós u
Mozsár u
Jókai tér
Oktogon
House of Terror
2
5
27
Ferenc Liszt Memorial Museum
Hunyadi tér
Szófia u
Király u
Jósika u

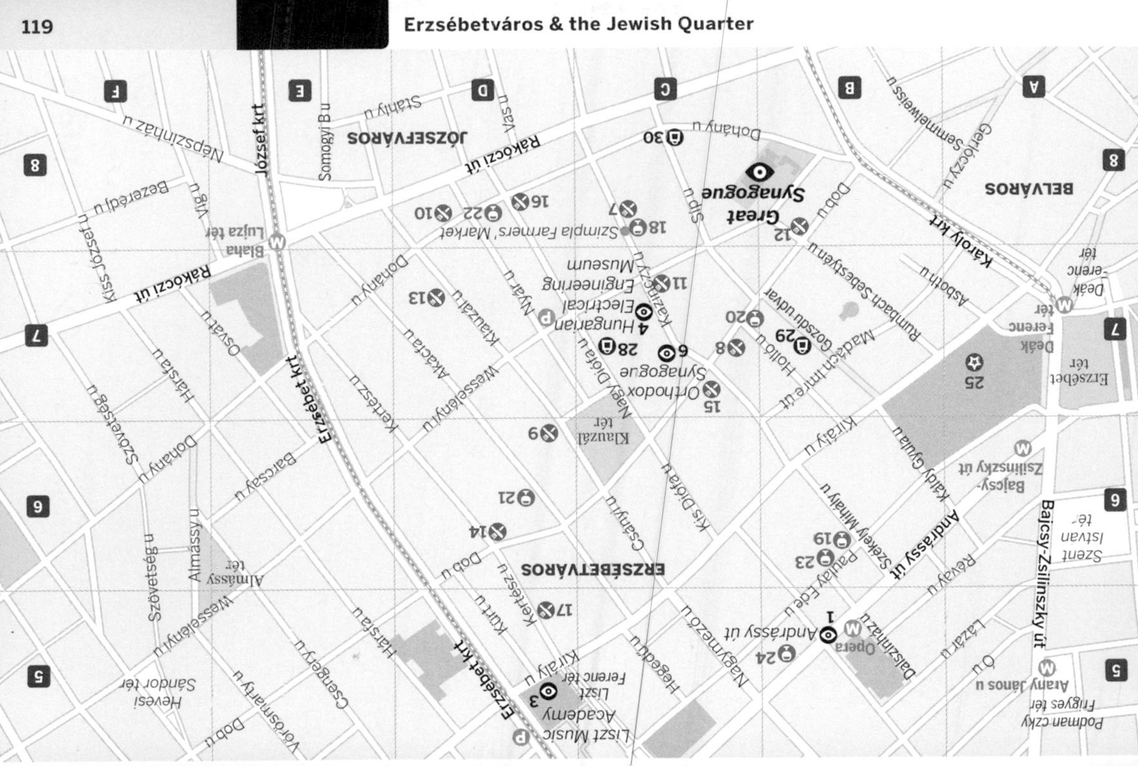
ERZSÉBETVÁROS
JÓZSEFVÁROS
BELVÁROS
Great Synagogue
Orthodox Synagogue
Hungarian Electrical Engineering Museum
Liszt Music Academy
Szimpla Farmers' Market
Liszt Ferenc tér
Klauzál tér
Almássy tér
Hevesi Sándor tér
Blaha Lujza tér
Erzsébet tér
Deák Ferenc tér
Szent István tér
Podmaniczky Frigyes tér
Opera
Arany János u
Bajcsy-Zsilinszky út
Andrássy út
Erzsébet krt
József krt
Károly krt
Rákóczi út
Dohány u
Wesselényi u
Király u
Dob u
Kazinczy u
Síp u
Rumbach Sebestyén u
Madách Imre út
Gozsdu udvar
Holló u
Nagy Diófa u
Kis Diófa u
Csányi u
Akácfa u
Klauzál u
Nyár u
Kertész u
Kürt u
Hársfa u
Csengery u
Vörösmarty u
Szövetség u
Almássy u
Barcsay u
Osvát u
Kiss József u
Bezerédj u
Víg u
Népszínház u
Somogyi B u
Stáhly u
Vas u
Semmelweiss u
Gerlóczy u
Asbóth u
Káldy Gyula u
Székely Mihály u
Paulay Ede u
Dalszínház u
Révay u
Lázár u
Ó u
Nagymező u
Hegedű u
A B C D E F
5 6 7 8

Sights

Andrássy Út

ARCHITECTURE

1 MAP P118, B5

Andrássy út starts a short distance northeast of Deák Ferenc tér and stretches for 2.5km, ending at Heroes' Sq (Hősök tere; p141) and the sprawling City Park (Városliget; p140). Listed by Unesco as a World Heritage Site in 2002, it is a tree-lined parade of knock-out architecture and is best enjoyed as a long stroll from the Hungarian State Opera House (p96) out to the park. (M M1 Opera)

House of Terror

MUSEUM

2 MAP P118, D3

The headquarters of the dreaded ÁVH secret police houses the disturbing House of Terror, focusing on the crimes and atrocities of Hungary's fascist and Stalinist regimes in a permanent exhibition called Double Occupation. But the years after WWII leading up to the 1956 Uprising get the lion's share of the exhibition space (almost three-dozen spaces on three levels). The reconstructed prison cells in the basement and the Perpetrators' Gallery on the staircase, featuring photographs of the turncoats, spies and torturers, are chilling. (Terror Háza; 1-374 2600; www.terrorhaza.hu; VI Andrássy út 60; adult/concession 3000/1500Ft, audio guide 1500Ft; 10am-6pm Tue-Sun; M M1 Vörösmarty utca, 4, 6)

Liszt Music Academy

NOTABLE BUILDING

3 MAP P118, D5

The art nouveau Liszt Music Academy, built in 1907, attracts students from all over the world and is Budapest's top **classical-music concert hall** (box office 1-321 0690; www.zeneakademia.hu; 1400-19,800Ft; box office 10am-6pm). The renovated interior, which has two concert halls and is richly embellished with Zsolnay porcelain and frescoes, is worth visiting on a guided tour if you're not attending a performance. (Liszt Zeneakadémia; 1-462 4600; www.zeneakademia.hu; VI Liszt Ferenc tér 8; adult/concession 3500/1750Ft; daily tours 1.30pm; M M1 Oktogon, 4, 6)

Hungarian Electrical Engineering Museum

MUSEUM

4 MAP P118, C7

This place might not sound like everyone's cup of tea, but some of the exhibits are unusual (and quirky) enough to warrant a visit. The staff will also show you how the alarm system of the barbed-wire fence between Hungary and Austria worked before the fall of communism, and there's also an exhibit on the nesting platforms that the electricity company kindly builds for storks throughout the country, so they won't interfere with the wires and electrocute themselves. (Magyar Elektrotechnikai Múzeum; 1-342 5750; http://

elektromuzeum.hu/hu; VII Kazinczy utca 21; adult/student & senior/family 800/400/1500Ft; 10am-5pm Tue-Fri, to 4pm Sat; trolleybus 74, M M2 Astoria)

Ferenc Liszt Memorial Museum MUSEUM

5 MAP P118, D3

This wonderful little museum is housed in the **Old Music Academy**, where the great composer Liszt lived in a 1st-floor apartment for five years until his death in 1886. The three rooms are filled with his pianos (including a tiny glass one), portraits and personal effects – all original. Concerts (adult/student and senior 2000/1000Ft or 2000/1500Ft with a museum visit) are usually held in the Chamber Hall at 11am on Saturday. (Liszt Ferenc Emlékmúzeum; 1-322 9804; www.lisztmuseum.hu; VI Vörösmarty utca 35; adult/student & senior 2000/1000Ft; 10am-6pm Mon-Fri, 9am-5pm Sat; M M1 Vörösmarty utca)

Orthodox Synagogue SYNAGOGUE

6 MAP P118, C7

Once one of a half-dozen synagogues and prayer houses in the Jewish Quarter, the Orthodox Synagogue was built in 1913 in what was at the time a very modern design. It has late art nouveau touches and is decorated in bright colours throughout. The stained-glass windows in the ceiling were designed by Miksa Róth, although those you see today are reconstructions, as the

House of Terror

POSZTOS / SHUTTERSTOCK ©

Little Underground

The **M1 metro** (aka Kisföldalatti or 'Little Underground'), which runs just below Andrássy út from Deák Ferenc tér as far as City Park, sticks to its side of the road below the surface and there's no interchange between the two sides. So, if you're heading north, board the trains on the east side of Andrássy út; for points south, go to the west side. Also possibly confusing is that one station is called Vörösmarty tér and another, five stops away, is Vörösmarty utca.

originals were bombed during WWII. (Ortodox zsinagóga; 1-351 0524; www.kazinczyutcaizsinagoga.hu; VII Kazinczy utca 29-31; 1000Ft; 10am-6pm Sun-Thu, to 4pm Fri Apr-Oct, 10am-4pm Sun-Thu, to 1pm Fri Nov-Mar; M M2 Astoria, 47, 49)

Eating

Bors GasztroBár SANDWICHES €

7 MAP P118, C8

We (and the rest of the world) love this thimble-sized place, not just for its hearty, imaginative soups but also for its equally good grilled baguettes: try 'Bors Dog' (spicy sausage and cheese) or their pulled pork. It's not a sit-down kind of place; most chow down on the pavement outside. (www.facebook.com/BorsGasztroBar; VII Kazinczy utca 10; soups 650Ft, baguettes 750-980Ft; 11.30am-9pm; M M2 Astoria)

Fröhlich Cukrászda CAFE, JEWISH €

8 MAP P118, C7

This kosher cake shop and cafe in the former ghetto, dating back to 1953, makes and sells such Jewish kosher favourites as *flódni* (a three-layer cake with apple, walnut and poppy-seed fillings; 480Ft) and *mákos kifli* (crescent-shaped biscuits stuffed with poppy seed; 330Ft). (1-266 1733; www.frohlich.hu; VII Dob utca 22; cakes & pastries 330-780Ft; 9am-6pm Mon-Thu, to 2pm Fri, 10am-6pm Sun; M M1/2/3 Deák Ferenc tér)

Kádár Étkezde HUNGARIAN €

9 MAP P118, D6

Located in the heart of the Jewish district, Kádár is one of the most popular and authentic *étkezdék* (canteens that serve simple dishes) you'll find in town and attracts the hungry with its ever-changing menu. Here you pay for everything: slices of bread, glasses of fizzy water from the seltzer bottle on the table etc. Find it on Facebook. (1-321 3622; X Klauzál tér 9; mains 1200-2500Ft; 11.30am-3.30pm Tue-Sat; M M2 Blaha Lujza tér, 4, 6)

ESCA Studio HUNGARIAN €€

10 MAP P118, D8

One of the best new modern Hungarian bistros, this place offers both excellent cooking and superb value. With internationally trained chef/owner Gábor Fehér at the helm, expect such 'oddities that work' as tomato soup with blueberry and red currants, and seared calves' feet with smoked mayonnaise. The place is small; be sure you book ahead, as lunch is only available if you have a reservation. (06 30 752 1509; http://escastudiorestaurant.hu; VII Dohány utca 29; 2-/3-/6-course menu 4500/8500/12,000Ft, with wine pairing 7500/13,500/19,000Ft; noon-3pm & 6-11pm; trolleybus 74, M2 Blaha Lujza tér, 4, 6)

Gettó Gulyás

HUNGARIAN €€

11 MAP P118, C7

This new spot is just about the best place to try *pörkölt* – what we call goulash (it's *paprikás* when you add sour cream) – with everything from chicken, venison and catfish to gizzards and roosters' testicles available. Add some *savanyúság* (pickled vegetables; from 480Ft) and you've got a feast. *Gulyás* in Hungary is a thickish beef soup (1200Ft). (06 20 376 4480; www.facebook.com/gettogulyas; VII Wesselényi utca 18; mains 2150-5650Ft; noon-11pm Sun-Thu, to midnight Fri & Sat; trolleybus 74, M2 Astoria, 47, 49)

Dobrumba

MEZZE €€

12 MAP P118, B8

This affable new restaurant in the heart of Party Town is a veritable geography lesson and a smorgasbord of tastes – from the Middle East and the Mediterranean to the Caucasus. But we look at it as a place for mezze (950Ft to 2600Ft) – cold ones like hummus and *muhammara* (red capsicum dip) and hot ones like *gambas piri piri* (prawns) and pomegranate chicken livers. (06 30 194 0049; https://dobrumba.hu; VII Dob utca 5; mains 2200-4800Ft; noon-midnight; M2 Astoria, 47, 49)

Barack & Szilva

HUNGARIAN €€

13 MAP P118, D7

This is the kind of perfectly formed restaurant that every neighbourhood wishes it could claim. Run by a friendly husband-and-wife team, the 'Peach & Plum' serves high-quality and exceptionally well-prepared Hungarian provincial food in a bistro setting. Try the duck pâté with dried plums (2970Ft) and the red-wine beef *pörkölt* (4200Ft). Lovely terrace in summer and live music, too. (Peach & Plum; 1-798 8285, 06 30 258 0965; www.barackesszilva.hu; VII Klauzál utca 13; mains 3300-6200Ft; 6pm-midnight Mon-Sat; trolleybus 74, M2 Blaha Lujza tér)

La Bodeguita del Medio

CUBAN €€

14 MAP P118, D6

Anchor tenant of the Fészek Club, meeting place of artists and intellectuals since 1901, La Bodeguita del Medio is a Cuban restaurant with such favourites as banana and yucca chips, *mantanzas* (a dish of grilled meats), *ropa vieja*

Farmers' Markets

Every Sunday, ruin pub **Szimpla Kert** (p125) holds a charming **farmers' market** (Szimplakerti Háztáji Piac; Map p118, C8; http://en.szimpla.hu/farmers-market; VII Kazinczy utca 14; 9am-2pm Sun; ; M2 Astoria) where you can buy all manner of local jams, honey, yoghurt, cheese and bread from between 30 and 40 producers. Also available are paprika, vegetables, fruit, cured meat and fruit juice. For organic produce, try the **MOM Park Organic Market** (MOM Park biopiac; 06 30 435 5680; www.facebook.com/mombiopiac; XII Csörsz utca 18; 6.30am-1pm Sat; 139, 56, 61) in Buda, set up every Saturday morning by local farmers and other growers.

(beef jerky) and a scrumptious tiger prawn and mango salad. It's in the city's most beautiful leafy courtyard. (06 20 388 2738; www.labodeguitadelmedio.hu; VII Dob utca 57; mains 2190-6490Ft; noon-1am Sun-Thu, to 3am Fri & Sat; 4, 6)

Kőleves JEWISH €€

15 MAP P118, C7

Always buzzy and lots of fun, the 'Stone Soup' attracts a young crowd with its Jewish-inspired (but not kosher) menu, lively decor, great service and reasonable prices. Good vegetarian choices. Breakfast (760Ft to 920Ft) is served from to 11am (11.30am at the weekend). The daily lunch is just 1350Ft (1200Ft for the vegetarian version). (1-322 1011, 06 20 213 5999; www.kolevesvendeglo.hu; VII Kazinczy utca 41; mains 2180-5080Ft; 8am-midnight Mon-Thu, 8am-1am Fri, 9am-1am Sat, 9am-midnight Sun; ; M1/2/3 Deák Ferenc tér)

Halkakas Halbistró SEAFOOD €€

16 MAP P118, D8

A charming 'fish bistro' now in the heart of the Jewish Quarter after a long stint off lower Váci utca, this place serves fresh, simple and great-value fish dishes such as catfish gyros platters, carp tempura with Asian cellophane noodles and fish 'n' chips. Relaxed and helpful service. Enter from Nagy Diófa utca. (06 30 226 0638; www.halkakas.hu; VII Dohány utca 36; mains 1750-3950Ft; noon-10pm Mon-Sat; trolleybus 74, M2 Blaha Kujza tér)

M Restaurant INTERNATIONAL €€

17 MAP P118, D5

A small, romantic spot with a laid-back vibe, brown-paper-bag decor and a short but very well thought-out menu of Hungarian dishes with a French twist like veal *onglet* steak (4400Ft) and duck breast with lentils (3300Ft). (06 31 783 0161, 1-322 3108; www.metterem.hu; VII Kertész utca 48; mains 2600-4600Ft; 6pm-midnight; ; M1 Oktogon, 4, 6)

Drinking

Szimpla Kert

RUIN PUB

18 MAP P118, C8

Budapest's first *romkocsma* (ruin pub), Szimpla Kert is firmly on the tourist trail but remains a landmark place for a drink. It's a huge complex with nooks that are filled with bric-a-brac, graffiti, art and all manner of unexpected items. Sit in an old Trabant car, watch a film outside in the open-air back courtyard, down shots or join in an acoustic jam session. (06 20 261 8669; http://en.szimpla.hu/szimpla-garden; VII Kazinczy utca 14; noon-4am Mon-Fri, 9am-4am Sat & Sun; M M2 Astoria)

Tuk Tuk Bar

GAY

19 MAP P118, B6

This 'Shanghai-inspired bar' – but aren't *tuk-tuks* (like the one on the pavement outside) from Bangkok, we cry? – is an ever-so-Asian gay hang-out at the Casati Budapest Hotel (p147). There's art on the walls, great cocktails, very friendly staff. (1-343 1198; www.tuktukbar.hu; VI Paulay Ede utca 31; 4pm-midnight; M M1 Opera)

Doblo

WINE BAR

20 MAP P118, C7

Brick-lined and candlelit, Doblo is where you go to taste Hungarian wines, with scores available by the 1.5cL (15mL) glass for 900Ft to 2150Ft. There's food such as meat and cheese platters, and

Szimpla Kert

live music nightly at 9pm. (06 20 398 8863; www.budapestwine.com; VII Dob utca 20; 2pm-2am Sun-Wed, to 4am Thu-Sat; M M1/2/3 Deák Ferenc tér)

Instant

CLUB

21 MAP P118, D6

We still love this 'ruin bar' even in its new location as part of the **Fogas** (06 70 638 5040; www.fogashaz.hu; VII Akácfa utca 49; 4pm-6am; ; trolleybus 70, 74, 78, 4, 6) stable and so do all our friends. It has a couple of dozen rooms to get lost in, seven bars, seven stages and two gardens, with underground DJs and dance parties. It's always heaving. (06 70 638 5040; www.instant.co.hu; VII Akácfa utca 51; 4pm-6am; trolleybus 70, 74, 78, 4, 6)

CoXx Men's Bar

GAY

22 MAP P118, D8

Probably the cruisiest gayme in town nowadays, this place with the in-your-face name has 400 sq metres of hunting ground, a mammoth bar and some significant play areas in back. Don't bring dark glasses. Find the bar on Facebook. (1-344 4884; VII Dohány utca 38; 9pm-4am Sun-Thu, to 5am Fri & Sat; M M2 Blaha Lujza tér, 4, 6)

Anker't

RUIN PUB

23 MAP P118, B6

Supposedly Budapest's largest outdoor beer garden, this achingly cool, grown-up courtyard pub surrounded by seriously ruined buildings has monochrome decor and lighting that sets off the impressive surrounds to great effect. There's a vast garden, numerous bars, food, a long drinks list, DJs and live music. Anker't is also a great dance venue. (06 30 360 3389; www.facebook.com/ankertbar; VI Paulay Ede utca 33; 2pm-midnight Sun-Tue, to 1am Wed, to 2am Thu, to 3am Fri & Sat; ; M M1 Opera)

Művész Kávéház

CAFE

24 MAP P118, B5

Diagonally opposite the Hungarian State Opera House, the 'Artist Coffee house' is an interesting place to people-watch (especially from the shady terrace), though some say its cakes (890Ft to 900Ft) are not what they used to be. (Presumably they're not thinking as far back as 1898, when the cafe opened.) (1-343 3544, 06 70 333 2116; www.muveszkavehaz.hu; VI Andrássy út 29; 8am-9pm Mon-Sat, 9am-9pm Sun; M M1 Opera)

Entertainment

Gödör Klub

LIVE MUSIC

25 MAP P118, A7

In the bowels of the Central Passage shopping centre on Király utca, Gödör has maintained its reputation for scheduling an excellent variety of indie, rock, jazz, electronic and experimental music, as well as hosting quality club nights in its spare, industrial space. Exhibitions and movies in summer, too. (06 20 201 3868; www.godorklub.hu; VI Király utca 8-10, Central Passage; 6pm-2am Mon-Wed, to 4am Thu-Sat; ; M1/2/3 Deák Ferenc tér)

Pótkulcs

LIVE MUSIC

26 MAP P118, C2

The 'Spare Key' is a fine little drinking venue with a varied menu of live music most evenings and occasional *táncház* (Hungarian music and dance). The small central courtyard is a wonderful place to chill out in summer. (1-269 1050; www.potkulcs.hu; VI Csengery utca 65/b; 5pm-1.30am Sun-Wed, to 2.30am Thu-Sat; M3 Nyugati pályaudvar)

Budapest Puppet Theatre

PUPPET THEATRE

27 MAP P118, D3

The city's puppet theatre presents puppet shows that are designed for children – show times are at 10am or 10.30am, and 2.30pm or 3pm. Performances usually don't require fluency in Hungarian to understand the show. Consult the theatre's website for the program schedules and exact puppet-show performance times. (Budapest Bábszínház; 1-461 5090, box office 1-342 2702; www.budapest-babszinhaz.hu; VI Andrássy út 69-71; tickets 1600-2300Ft; box office 9am-6pm; M1 Vörösmarty utca)

Shopping

Massolit Books & Cafe

BOOKS

28 MAP P118, C7

A branch of the celebrated bookshop in Kraków, Massolit is one of Budapest's best, with new and secondhand English-language fiction and nonfiction, including Hungarian history and literature in translation. It has a shady little back garden and tables set among the shelves, so you can enjoy coffee, bagels and cakes as you browse the volumes. (1-788 5292; www.facebook.com/MassolitBudapest; VII Nagy Diófa utca 30; 8am-7.30pm Mon-Sat, from 10am Sun; M2 Astoria)

Gouba Gozsdu Bazaar

MARKET

29 MAP P118, B7

A Sunday arts and crafts market where you can pick up interesting pieces from local artists and designers. It's a good place to shop for souvenirs, too. (www.gouba.hu; VII Gozsdu udvar, VII Király utca 13 & Dob utca 16; 10am-7pm Sun; M1/2/3 Deák Ferenc tér)

Szputnyik Shop D-20

FASHION & ACCESSORIES

30 MAP P118, C8

A bright, open space, stuffed with vintage fashion like US college jackets and Converse sneakers, plus a selection of new alternative lines from international designers. (1-321 3730; http://szputnyikshop.hu; VII Dohány utca 20; 10am-8pm Mon-Sat, to 6pm Sun; M2 Astoria)

Southern Pest

The colourful districts of Józsefváros (Joseph Town) and Ferencváros (Francis, or Franz, Town) – no prizes for guessing which Habsburg emperors these were named after – are traditionally working class and full of students. It's a lot of fun wandering the backstreets, peeping into courtyards and small, often traditional, shops. Both are evolving areas, though, with new shops, bars and restaurants popping up everywhere.

The Short List

- ***Hungarian National Museum (p130)*** *Taking a trip through the past by wandering the corridors of this treasure trove of history.*
- ***Nagycsarnok (p133)*** *Strolling through the well-endowed Great Market Hall, with its excellent selection of folkcraft and comestibles.*
- ***Museum of Applied Arts (p135)*** *Admiring the architecture of this striking art nouveau palace with its majestic maiolica-tiled roof.*
- ***Kerepes Cemetery (p135)*** *Paying your respects to the great and the good, statesmen and heroes of the 1956 Uprising buried here.*

Getting There & Around

M The red M2 line runs along the northern border of Józsefváros, while the blue M3 line serves points in Ferencváros. The green M4 line handily connects Fővám tér with Keleti pályaudvar.

Both districts are served by trams 47 and 49, and further east by trams 4 and 6.

Southern Pest Map on p134

Zwack Museum & Visitors' Centre (p136) POSZTOS / SHUTTERSTOCK ©

Top Sight

Hungarian National Museum

The Hungarian National Museum houses the nation's most important collection of historical relics. It traces the history of the Carpathian Basin from the Stone Age, and that of the Magyar people and Hungary from the 9th-century conquest to the end of communism. The museum was founded in 1802 when Count Ferenc Széchényi donated his personal collection to the state.

MAP P134, B2

Magyar Nemzeti Múzeum

www.hnm.hu

VIII Múzeum körút 14-16

10am-6pm Tue-Sun

M3/4 Kálvin tér, 47, 49

Front Steps

Less than a year after it moved into its new premises, an impressive neoclassical building designed by Mihály Pollack in 1847, the museum was the scene of a momentous event. On 15 March a crowd gathered to hear the poet Sándor Petőfi recite his 'Nemzeti Dal' (National Song) from the front steps, sparking the 1848–49 revolution.

History Exhibitions

On the museum's 1st floor, exhibits look at the history of the Carpathian Basin from prehistory to the 9th-century arrival of the Magyars. On the floor above they continue from the Árpád Dynasty to the fall of communism. In the basement there is a Roman lapidary including a stunning 2nd-century mosaic from Balácapuszta near Veszprém north of Lake Balaton.

Coronation Mantle

In its own room to the left as you ascend the massive staircase to the 1st floor, you'll find King Stephen's beautiful crimson silk coronation mantle, stitched by nuns in 1031. It was refashioned in the 13th century and the much-faded cloth features an intricate embroidery of fine gold thread and pearls.

Museum Gardens

You may enjoy walking around the museum gardens, laid out in 1856 and recently given a massive new layout. The Roman column to the left of the museum entrance once stood in the Forum and was a gift from Mussolini. Among the monuments is a statue of János Arany (1817–82), author of the epic *Toldi Trilogy*. There's also a Soviet tank dating from the 1956 Uprising.

★ Top Tips

- Audio guides for the permanent collection are available in four languages including English for 750Ft for the first hour and 250Ft after that.
- The museum shop sells excellent reproductions of 3rd-century Celtic gold and silver jewellery.

✕ Take a Break

The **Építész Pince** (www.epiteszpince.hu; VIII Ötpacsirta utca 2; mains 2200-4100Ft; ⌚11am-10pm Mon-Thu, to midnight Fri & Sat; 📶) just round the corner serves a bargain set lunch (1150Ft) from Monday to Friday.

For just a drink, head southeast to Mikszáth Kálmán tér and **Lumen Kávézó** (☎1-781 5156; www.facebook.com/lumen.kavezo; VIII Mikszáth Kálmán tér 2-3; ⌚8am-midnight Mon-Fri, 10am-midnight Sat, 10am-10pm Sun) for excellent coffee and craft beers.

Walking Tour

From Market to Market

The ideal way to appreciate these two fascinating but large traditionally working-class districts is to pick a sight and then spend some time wandering in the nearby streets. This area, set between excellent markets, is filled with antiquarian bookshops, ghosts from the 1956 Uprising, unusual architecture, and trendy bars and restaurants.

Getting There

Ⓜ Lines M3 and M4 serve IX Kálvin tér; VIII Rákóczi tér is on the M4.

🚊 Trams 47 and 49 run along the Little Ring Road, the 4 and 6 on the Big Ring Road.

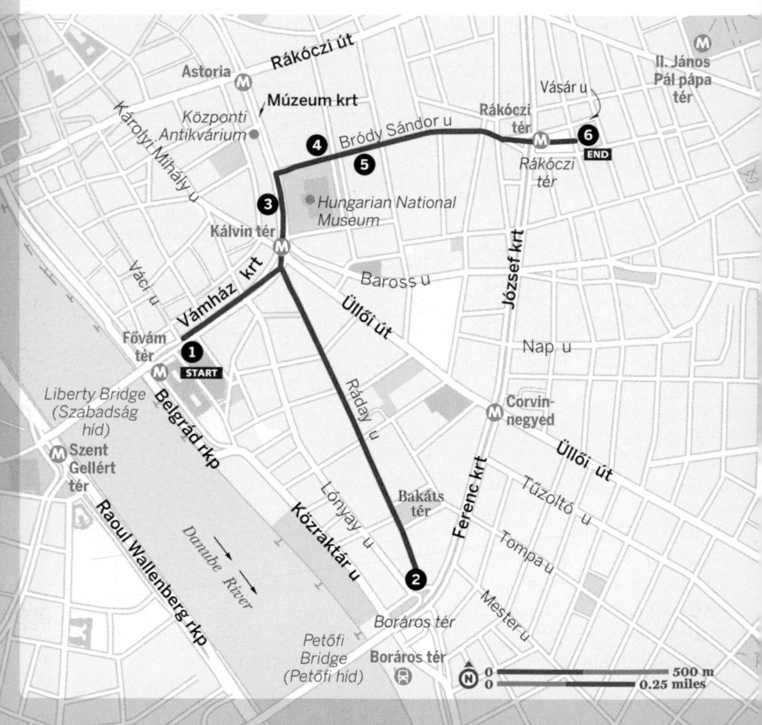

❶ Nagycsarnok

The **Nagycsarnok** (Great Market Hall; ☎1-366 3300; www.piaconline.hu; IX Vámház körút 1-3; ⏰6am-5pm Mon, to 6pm Tue-Fri, to 3pm Sat; Ⓜ M4 Fővám tér, 🚋47, 49) is Budapest's largest market. It might attract tourists in droves, but it's a great place for one-stop shopping. You'll find a number of local food products here for less than you'd pay in Váci utca shops – shrink-wrapped and potted foie gras, garlands of dried paprika, souvenir sacks and tins of paprika powder, all kinds of honey.

❷ Brunch Break

Ráday utca, a long strip whose pavement tables fill with diners on warm summer days, is a lively place to head to in this district at any time of day. Stop for brunch at **Jedermann Cafe** (☎06 30 406 3617; www.jedermann.hu; XI Ráday utca 58; ⏰8am-1am; 🚋4, 6), an uber-chilled cafe and restaurant at the southern end of the street with an excellent weekday set lunch.

❸ Antiquarian Bookshops

The western side of Múzeum körút is lined with shops selling antiquarian and secondhand books. Our favourite is the **Múzeum Antikvárium** (www.muzeumantikvarium.hu; V Múzeum körút 35; ⏰10am-6pm Mon-Fri, to 2pm Sat; Ⓜ M3/4 Kálvin tér) just opposite the Hungarian National Museum. Further north is **Központi Antikvárium** (www.kozpontiantikvarium.hu; V Múzeum körút 13-15; ⏰10am-6pm Mon-Fri, to 2pm Sat; Ⓜ M2 Astoria), the largest and oldest in town.

❹ Brody House

Now a fancy-schmancy **hotel** (☎1-550 7363; www.brody.land; VIII Bródy Sándor utca 10; r €80-120; ❄@📶; Ⓜ M3 Kálvin tér, 🚋47, 49), Brody House would have lots of tales to tell, could it speak. It was the residence of Hungary's prime minister in the 19th century when Parliament sat next door at No 8. And if you don't believe that, just look at the verso of the 20,000Ft note.

❺ Hungarian Radio Headquarters

On the evening of 23 October 1956, ÁVH government agents fired on a group of protesters gathering outside these **radio headquarters** (Magyar Rádió; VIII Bródy Sándor utca 5-7; Ⓜ M3 Kálvin tér, 🚋47, 49) when they began shouting anti-Soviet slogans and demanding that reformist Imre Nagy be named prime minister. By morning Budapest was in revolution.

❻ Rákóczi Tér Market

Finish your walk at this handsome and very authentic **market hall** (Rákóczi téri piac; www.piaconline.hu; VIII Rákóczi tér 7-9; ⏰6am-4pm Mon, to 6pm Tue-Fri, to 1pm Sat; Ⓜ M4 Rákóczi tér, 🚋4, 6) dating from 1897. Inside you'll find all the usual staples – fruit, veg, cured meats, cheese, jam and baked goods – and some folk bring their goods in direct from the farm.

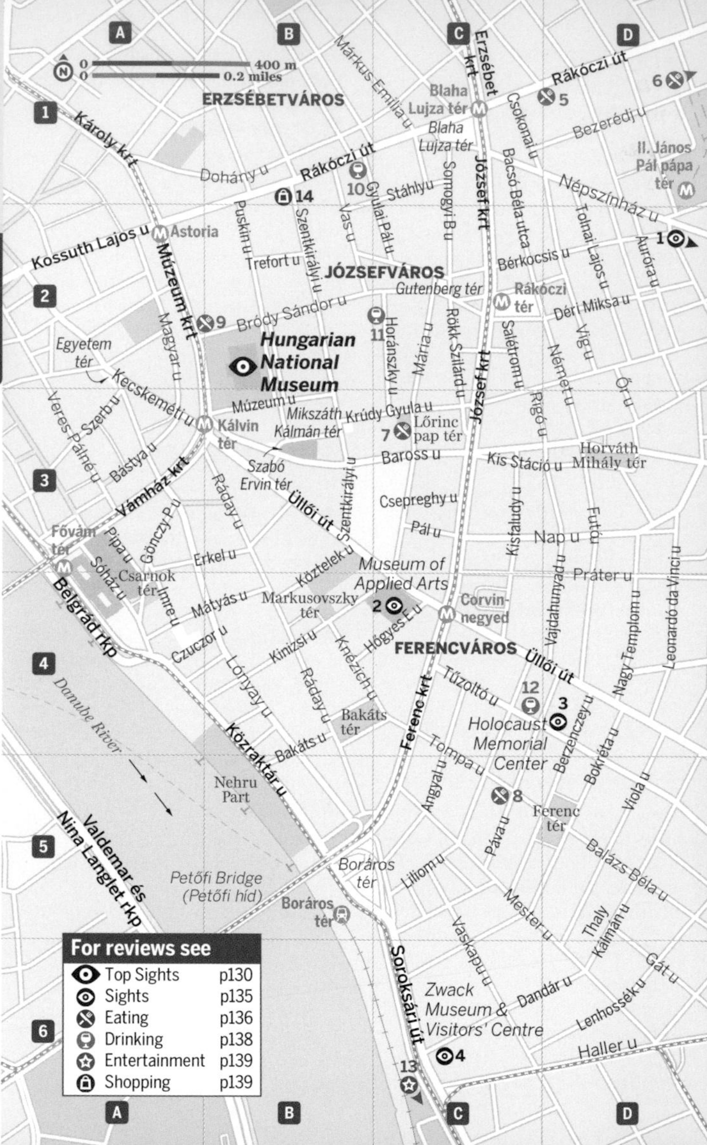
A
B
C
D
1
2
3
4
5
6
0 400 m
0 0.2 miles
ERZSÉBETVÁROS
JÓZSEFVÁROS
FERENCVÁROS
Károly krt
Kossuth Lajos u
Astoria
Múzeum krt
Dohány u
Rákóczi út
14
10
Márkus Emília u
Erzsébet krt
Blaha Lujza tér
Blaha Lujza tér
Csokonai u
5
6
Bezerédj u
II. János Pál pápa tér
Népszínház u
1
Puskin u
Szentkirályi u
Vas u
Gyulai Pál u
Stáhly u
Somogyi B u
József krt
Bacsó Béla utca
Tolnai Lajos u
Auróra u
Trefort u
Bérkocsis u
Gutenberg tér
Rákóczi tér
Déri Miksa u
Egyetem tér
Magyar u
9
Bródy Sándor u
11
Hungarian National Museum
Horánszky u
Mária u
Rökk Szilárd u
Salétrom u
Német u
Vig u
Kecskeméti u
Veres Pálné u
Szerb u
Múzeum u
Mikszáth Kálmán tér
Krúdy Gyula u
7
Lőrinc pap tér
Rigó u
Őr u
Kálvin tér
Bástya u
Vámház krt
Szabó Ervin tér
Baross u
Kis Stáció u
Horváth Mihály tér
Ráday u
Üllői út
Csepreghy u
Kisfaludy u
Fővám tér
Pipa u
Gönczy P u
Pál u
Nap u
Futó u
Leonardo da Vinci u
Sóház u
Csarnok tér
Erkel u
Köztelek u
Museum of Applied Arts
Práter u
Belgrád rkp
Imre u
Mátyás u
Markusovszky tér
2
Hőgyes E u
Corvin-negyed
Vajdahunyad u
Czuczor u
Kinizsi u
Knézich u
FERENCVÁROS
Üllői út
Nagy Templom u
Danube River
Lónyay u
Ráday u
Ferenc krt
Tűzoltó u
12
3
Holocaust Memorial Center
Berzenczey u
Bakáts tér
Bakáts u
Tompa u
Bokréta u
Közraktár u
Nehru Part
Angyal u
8
Ferenc tér
Viola u
Páva u
Valdemar és Nina Langlet rkp
Petőfi Bridge (Petőfi híd)
Boráros tér
Liliom u
Balázs Béla u
Boráros tér
Mester u
Thaly Kálmán u
Vaskapu u
Soroksári út
Gát u
Zwack Museum & Visitors' Centre
Dandár u
Lenhossék u
4
Haller u
13
For reviews see
Top Sights p130
Sights p135
Eating p136
Drinking p138
Entertainment p139
Shopping p139

Sights

Kerepes Cemetery

CEMETERY

1 MAP P134, D2

Also known as the Fiume St Graveyard (Fiumei uti sírkert), this is Budapest's equivalent of London's Highgate or Père Lachaise in Paris. Established in 1847, this 56-hectare necropolis holds some 3000 gravestones and mausoleums, including those of statesmen and national heroes Lajos Kossuth, Ferenc Deák and Lajos Batthyány. Plot 21 contains the graves of many who died in the 1956 Uprising. Maps indicating the location of noteworthy graves are available free at the entrance. (Kerepesi temető; 1-896 3891; www.fiumeiutisirkert.nori.gov.hu; VIII Fiumei út 16; admission free; 7am-8pm May-Jul, to 7pm Apr & Aug, to 6pm Sep, to 5pm Mar & Oct, 7.30am-5pm Nov-Feb; M M2/4 Keleti train station, 24)

Museum of Applied Arts

MUSEUM

2 MAP P134, C4

Housed in a gorgeous Ödön Lechner–designed building (1896) decorated with Zsolnay ceramic tiles, this museum was closed for renovation at the time of research and was not due to reopen till early 2021. Its main collection contains Hungarian and European furniture from the 18th and 19th centuries, art nouveau and Secessionist artefacts, and objects relating to trades and

Kerepes Cemetery

crafts (glassmaking, bookbinding, goldsmithing). Another one consists of Islamic art and artefacts from the 9th to the 19th centuries. (Iparművészeti Múzeum; 1-456 5107; www.imm.hu; IX Üllői út 33-37; adult/student 2000/1000Ft, with temporary exhibitions 3500/1750Ft; 10am-6pm Tue-Sun; M3 Corvin-negyed, 4, 6)

Holocaust Memorial Center JEWISH SITE

3 MAP P134, D4

Housed in a striking modern building, the centre opened in 2004 on the 60th anniversary of the start of the Holocaust in Hungary. The thematic permanent exhibition traces the rise of anti-Semitism in Hungary and follows the path to genocide of Hungary's Jewish and Roma communities. A sublimely restored synagogue in the central courtyard, designed by Leopold Baumhorn and completed in 1924, hosts temporary exhibitions. An 8m-high wall nearby bears the names of Hungarian victims of the Holocaust. (Holokauszt Emlékközpont; 1-455 3333; www.hdke.hu; IX Páva utca 39; adult/concession 1400/700Ft; 10am-6pm Tue-Sun; M3 Corvin-negyed, 4, 6)

Zwack Museum & Visitors' Centre MUSEUM

4 MAP P134, C6

Unicum, the thick medicinal-tasting aperitif made from 40 herbs and spices, is as bitter as a loser's tears and a favourite drink in Hungary. To delve into its history, head for this small museum, which starts with a rather schmaltzy video, has an enormous collection of 17,000 miniatures from across the globe and concludes with an educated tasting session. You can buy more from the adjacent shop open 9am to 6pm weekdays and from 10am on Saturday. (Zwack Múzeum és Látogatóközpont; 1-476 2383; www.zwackunicum.hu/en; IX Dandár utca 1; adult/under 18yr 2200/1100Ft; 10am-5pm Mon-Sat; 2, 24)

Eating

Hauer Cukrászda és Kávéház CAFE €

5 MAP P134, D1

This historic (and enormous) confectionery first opened in 1899 but changed names and direction after WWII and only regained its former fin-de-siècle glory with mirror-lined walls, plush red-velvet carpets and white-marble tables – not to mention the collection of scrumptious classic cakes – in 2016. (1-612 1313; www.facebook.com/pg/hauercukraszda; VIII Rákóczi útca 47-49; cakes 590-890Ft; 8am-8pm; M2 Blaha Lujza tér, 4, 6)

Rosenstein HUNGARIAN €€

6 MAP P134, D1

A top-notch and cosy Hungarian restaurant in an unlikely location, with Jewish tastes and super service. Family-run – the owner is also the chef – it has been here for

DIRK RENCKHOFF / IMAGEBROKER / AGE FOTOSTOCK ©

Synagogue at Holocaust Memorial Center

years, so expect everyone to know each other. The extensive menu features some interesting game dishes. Try their own version of plum *pálinka* (fruit brandy). (1-333 3492; www.rosenstein.hu; VIII Mosonyi utca 3; mains 2800-6500Ft; noon-11pm Mon-Sat; M M2/4 Keleti train station, 24)

Alma & Körte

HUNGARIAN €€

7 MAP P134, C3

Sister-restaurant to the wonderful Barack & Szilva (Peach & Peach; p123) in Erzsébetváros (the restaurant names have more to do with *pálinka* than fruit), this place serves Hungarian classics like catfish stew and exceptional roast rabbit in a newer and lighter fashion. We love the old-style ladder suspended over the bar and hung with old farm implements. (Apple & Pear; 06 30 667 0822, 1-786 7803; www.facebook.com/almaandkorte; VIII Lőrinc pap tér 3; mains 3100-5500Ft; 6pm-midnight Tue-Sat; M M3 Corvin-negyed, M3/4 Kálvin tér, 4, 6)

Paletta Bistró

HUNGARIAN €€

8 MAP P134, C5

This new kid on the block in Southern Pest – a transplant from Keszthely on the Balaton – has a lakeside vibe, with whitewashed clapboard terrace, lots of blues and the odd nautical hint. The menu is enlightened and inspired with things like smoked carp ramen (1950Ft). But their signature dish is every Hungarian kid's favourite food: *rántott sajt* (breaded and deep-fried cheese; 3350Ft). (06 70 947 4985;

www.palettabisztro.hu; IX Tompa utca 28; mains 2450-5350Ft; ⌚11.30am-10pm Mon-Sat, 9am-4pm Sun)

Múzeum

HUNGARIAN €€€

9  MAP P134, B2

This very suave restaurant is the place to come if you like to dine in old-world style with a piano softly tinkling in the background. It's still going strong after almost 135 years at the same location. The goose-liver parfait (3600Ft) is to die for, the goose leg and cabbage (4400Ft) and roasted *fogas* (pike-perch) iconic. There is also a well-chosen selection of Hungarian wines. (☎1-338 4221, 1-267 0375; www.muzeumkavehaz.hu; VIII Múzeum körút 12; mains 3400-7400Ft; ⌚6pm-midnight Mon-Sat; Ⓜ M3/4 Kálvin tér, 🚊47, 49)

Élesztő

HEMIS / ALAMY STOCK PHOTO ©

Drinking

Neked Csak Dezső!

CRAFT BEER

10 MAP P134, B1

This temple to craft beer, which takes its odd name from the eponymous slaughtered pig (note the wooden portrait on the wall) in the iconic Hungarian 1969 film *A Tanú* (The Witness), has 32 taps a-flowing, with such essential local IPAs and lagers as Horizont, Mad Scientist and four of their own brewed in-house. Great place to start (or end) an evening. (You're only Dezső!; ☎06 30 177 7424, 06 20 316 0931; www.nekedcsak.hu; VIII Rákóczi út 29; ⌚9am-midnight Sun-Tue, to 1am Wed, to 2am Thu-Sat)

Lumen Café

BAR

11 MAP P134, C2

This enormous venue with multiple rooms, including covered and open courtyards facing a huge brick smoke stack of what was once a pipe factory, does breakfast (1250Ft to 1950Ft), sandwiches and more elaborate mains (1450Ft to 2650Ft). But come here mostly to drink and listen to music (traditional and experimental jazz, pop, world) from 8pm Tuesday to Saturday. (☎06 20 402 2393; www.facebook.com/lumen.kavezo; VIII Horánszky utca 5; ⌚8am-midnight Mon-Fri, 10am-midnight Sat & Sun; Ⓜ M4 Rákóczi tér)

Élesztő

CRAFT BEER

12 MAP P134, C4

This ruin pub, set in a former glass-blowing workshop, has three sections: a cafe, a wine bar with tapas (890Ft to 1390Ft) and the reason we come...a bar with an unrivalled selection of craft beer. With a brewery on-site and a name meaning 'yeast', 30 brews on tap, beer cocktails and brewing courses, this is a hophead's dream. (www.facebook.com/elesztohaz; IX Tűzoltó utca 22; 3pm-3am; M M3 Corvin-negyed, 4, 6)

Entertainment

Palace of Arts

CONCERT VENUE

13 MAP P134, C6

The two concert halls at this palatial arts centre by the Danube are the 1700-seat **Béla Bartók National Concert Hall** (Bartók Béla Nemzeti Hangversenyterem) and the smaller **Festival Theatre** (Fesztivál Színház), accommodating up to 450 people. Both are purported to have near-perfect acoustics. Students can pay 500Ft one hour before performances for a standing-only ticket. (Művészetek Palotája (Müpa); box office 1-555 3300; www.mupa.hu; IX Komor Marcell utca 1; box office 10am-6pm; ; 2, 24, (HÉV) H7 Közvágóhíd)

Tipples to Try

Don't leave Hungary without trying its two most famous spirits. *Pálinka*, a strong brandy or *eau de vie* distilled from a variety of fruits (most commonly apricots or plums), kicks like a mule and is served in most bars, some of which carry an enormous range. You'll also come to recognise Unicum and its unique medicinal-looking bottle. It's a bitter aperitif that has been around since 1790 and is now available in three different versions.

Shopping

Magyar Pálinka Háza

DRINKS

14 MAP P134, B1

This large shop stocks hundreds of varieties of *pálinka*. Szicsek and Prekop are premium brands. *Pálinka*-filled chocolates make for an unusual gift. (Hungarian Pálinka House; 06 70 934 0026, 06 30 421 5463; www.magyarpalinkahaza.hu; VIII Rákóczi út 17; 9am-7pm Mon-Sat; 7, M M2 Astoria)

Worth a Trip

City Park

City Park is a heavyweight when it comes to sights. Apart from one world-class art museum and a smaller one dedicated to contemporary art, there's also Budapest's most impressive square, the zoo, Széchenyi Baths and a fine 19th-century castle. A number of new attractions will include a biodome at the expanded zoo, and new homes for the Hungarian National Gallery and the Ethnography Museum.

Városliget

20E, 30, M M1 Hősök tere, Széchenyi fürdő, trolleybus 70, 72, 75, 79

Museum of Fine Arts

Housed in a grand Renaissance-style building and once again open after several years' renovations, the **Museum of Fine Arts** (Szépművészeti Múzeum; ☎1-469 7100; www.mfab.hu; XIV Dózsa György út 41; adult/concession 1400/700Ft; ⏰10am-6pm Tue-Sun; Ⓜ M1 Hősök tere) is home to the city's most outstanding collection of foreign works of art, ranging from articles from ancient Egypt to stellar collections of Spanish, Flemish, Italian and German art. It also now includes Hungarian art for the first time in four decades. The private collection of Count Miklós Esterházy, purchased by the state in 1870, forms the nucleus of the collection.

Széchenyi Baths

The gigantic 'wedding cake' of a building in City Park dates from just before the outbreak of WWI and houses the **Széchenyi Baths** (Széchenyi Gyógyfürdő; ☎1-363 3210, 06 30 462 8236; www.szechenyibath.hu; XIV Állatkerti körút 9-11; tickets incl locker/cabin Mon-Fri 5200/5700Ft, Sat & Sun 5400/5900Ft; ⏰6am-10pm; Ⓜ M1 Széchenyi fürdő), whose hot-water spring was discovered while a well was being drilled in the late 19th century. It also stands out for its immensity; it's the largest medicinal bath extant in Europe, with 15 indoor pools and three outdoor.

Heroes' Square & Millenary Monument

Heroes' Square is the largest and most symbolic square in Budapest, and contains the **Millenary Monument** (Ezeréves emlékmű), a 36m-high pillar topped by a golden Archangel Gabriel. Legend has it that the Archangel Gabriel offered Stephen the crown of Hungary in a dream. At the column's base are Prince Árpád and six other chieftains. The colonnades that are located behind the pillar feature various

★ Top Tip

- For lofty views of the park's iconic architecture and beyond, it's well worth taking a guided tour up the **Apostles' Tower** (Apostolok Tornya; Vajdahunyadvár; 600Ft; ⏰10am-5pm Tue-Sun Mar-Oct, 10am-4pm Tue-Fri, to 5pm Sat & Sun Nov-Feb; 🚎trolleybus 75, 79, Ⓜ M1 Széchenyi fürdő).

✕ Take a Break

If it's Sunday head for **Gundel** (☎06 30 603 2480; www.gundel.hu; XIV Gundel Károly út 4; mains 6200-29,000Ft, set lunch menus 6500-7900Ft, Sun brunch adult/child 9800/4900Ft; ⏰noon-11pm Sun-Thu, to midnight Fri & Sat; Ⓜ M1 Hősök tere) and its famous brunch. **Robinson** (☎06 30 663 6871; www.robinsonrestaurant.hu; XIV Városligeti-tó; mains 4500-12,900Ft; ⏰noon-4pm & 6-11pm; 🚎trolleybus 75, 79, Ⓜ M1 Hősök tere) is a good place for a lakeside drink or light meal anytime.

illustrious leaders of Hungary. It was designed in 1896 to mark the 1000th anniversary of the Magyar conquest of the Carpathian Basin.

Budapest Zoo

This **zoo** (Budapesti Állatkert; ☎1-273 4900; www.zoobudapest.com; XIV Állatkerti körút 6-12; adult/2-14yr/family 3000/2000/8400Ft; ⌚9am-6pm Mon-Thu, to 7pm Fri-Sun May-Aug, hours vary in other months; 👪; 🚌trolleybus 72, 75, 79, Ⓜ M1 Széchenyi fürdő), which opened with 500 animals in 1866, has an excellent collection of big cats, hippopotamuses, bears and giraffes, and some of the themed houses (eg Madagascar, wetlands, nocturnal Australia) are well executed, though water in ponds could be less stagnant. Have a look at the Secessionist animal houses that were built in the early part of the 20th century, such as the Elephant House with Zsolnay ceramics, and the Palm House with an aquarium erected by the Eiffel Company of Paris.

Palace of Art

The **Palace of Art** (Műczarnok; ☎1-460 7000; www.mucsarnok.hu; XIV Dózsa György út 37; adult/concession 1600/800Ft; ⌚10am-6pm Tue, Wed & Fri-Sun, noon-8pm Thu; 🚌20E, 30, Ⓜ M1 Hősök tere), reminiscent of a Greek temple, is among the city's largest exhibition spaces. It focuses on contemporary visual arts, with some three to four major exhibitions staged annually; recent exhibitions comprised cutting-edge photography, sculpture and installations by home-grown and international

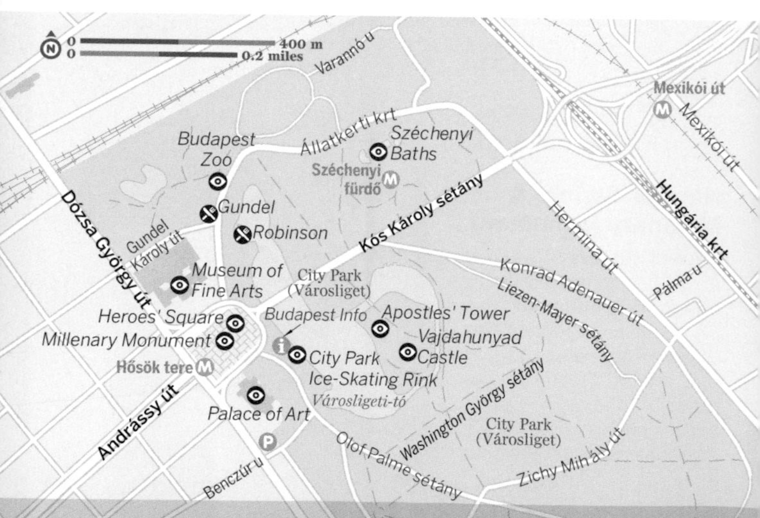

artists. Go for the scrumptious venue and the excellent museum shop. Concerts are sometimes staged here as well.

Vajdahunyad Castle

Erected for the 1896 millenary celebrations originally in canvas and later built in stone, the **castle** (pictured p140; Vajdahunyadvár; XIV Városliget; M M1 Széchenyi fürdő) was modelled after a fortress in Transylvania – but with Gothic, Romanesque and baroque wings, and additions to reflect architectural styles from all over Hungary.

Unknown Chronicler

The statue of the hooded figure opposite Vajdahunyad Castle is that of **Anonymous**, the unknown chronicler at the court of King Béla III who wrote a history of the early Magyars. Note the pen with the shiny tip in his hand; writers (both real and aspirant) stroke it for inspiration.

Survival Guide

Tram in motion along Liberty Bridge (p55) GEHRINGJ / GETTY IMAGES ©

Before You Go

Book Your Stay

Accommodation in Budapest runs the gamut from hostels in converted flats and private rooms in far-flung housing estates to luxury guesthouses in the Buda Hills and five-star properties charging upwards of €350 a night. In general, accommodation is more limited in the Buda neighbourhoods than on the other side of the Danube River in Pest.

Useful Websites

Best Hotel Service (www.besthotelservice.hu) Good for budget accommodation.

Discover Budapest (www.discoverbudapest.com) Tour company that also books accommodation.

Hip Homes Hungary (www.hiphomeshungary.com) Offers fabulous short-term apartments.

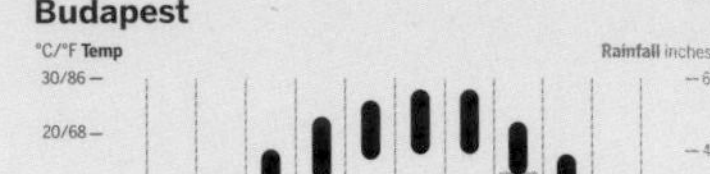
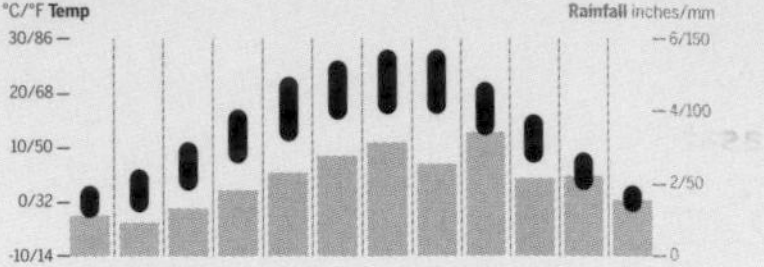

When to Go

○ Spring (Apr–Jun) Often wet, but just glorious, with fewer tourists.

○ Summer (Jul & Aug) Warm, sunny and unusually long. Expect higher prices and long queues.

○ Autumn (Sep & Oct) Beautiful, particularly in the Buda Hills; festivals mark the *szüret* (grape harvest).

○ Winter (Nov–Mar) Can be cold and bleak; some attractions curtail their hours or shut entirely till mid-March.

Lonely Planet (lonelyplanet.com/hungary/budapest#lodgings) Recommendations and bookings.

Mellow Mood Group (www.mellowmood.hu) Chain with a big variety of options.

Best Budget

Maverick City Lodge (☎1-793 1605; www.mavericklodges.com; Kazinczy utca 24-26; dm from €10-22, d €40-70; @ 📶; M M2 Astoria) Modern, warehouse-style hostel with great facilities.

Shantee House (☎06 30 402 0328, 1-385 8946; www.shanteehouse.com; XI Takács Menyhért utca 33; beds in yurt €10-13, large/small dm from €11/14, d €32-55; P @ 📶; 🚌7, 153, 🚋19, 49) Budapest's first hostel grows (up) in size and design.

Zen House (☎06 30 688 7599; www.zenhouse-budapest.com; III Repkény utca 11; r/tr €27/32; 📶; 🚌29, 🚋17, 19, 41, 🚍Szépvölgyi út) Family-run place offering stylish private rooms.

Best Midrange

Baltazár (☎1-300 7051; http://baltazarbudapest.com; I Országház utca 31;

r/ste from €170/240; ❄ 📶; 🚌 16, 16A, 116) Midrange hotel with a high-end Castle location.

Casati Budapest Hotel (☎ 1-343 1198; www.casatibudapesthotel.com; VI Paulay Ede utca 31; r €90-140; P ❄ 📶; M M1 Opera) Artful conversion of a beautiful building with sustainable credentials

Hotel Papillon (☎ 1-212 4750; www.hotelpapillon.hu; II Rózsahegy utca 3/b; s/d/tr €49/69/75, apt €84-99; P ❄ 📶 🏊; 🚋 4, 6) Delightful 'country-style' hotel in the Buda Hills.

Best Top End

Art'otel Budapest (☎ 1-487 9487; www.artotels.com/budapest-hotel-hu-h-1011/hunbuart; I Bem rakpart 16-19; r/ste from €150/200; P ❄ 📶; 🚋 19, 41) Über-designed caravanserai hard by the Danube.

Hotel Palazzo Zichy (☎ 1-235 4000; www.hotel-palazzo-zichy.hu; VIII Lőrinc pap tér 2; r/ste from €110/160; P ❄ @ 📶; M M3 Corvin-negyed, M3/4 Kálvin tér, 🚋 4, 6) Impressive palace hotel on a lovely little square.

Arriving in Budapest

Ferenc Liszt International Airport

Minibuses, buses and trains to central Budapest run from 4.30am to 11.50pm (700Ft to 2000Ft); taxis cost from 6000Ft.

Keleti, Nyugati & Déli Train Stations

Keleti, Nyugati and Déli train stations are all connected to metro lines of the same names, and night bus services run from the train stations when the metro services are closed.

Népliget & Stadion Bus Stations

Both bus stations are on metro lines (M3 and M2 respectively) and are served by tram 1.

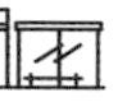

Getting Around

Metro

Budapest has four underground metro lines. Three of them converge at Deák Ferenc tér (only): the little yellow (or Millennium) line designated the M1 that runs from Vörösmarty tér to Mexikói út in Pest; the red M2 line from Déli train station in Buda to Örs vezér tere in Pest; and the blue M3 line from Újpest-Központ to Kőbánya-Kispest in Pest. The new green M4 metro runs from Kelenföldi train station in southern Buda to Keleti train station in Pest, where it links with the M2. It links with the M3 at Kálvin tér. All four metro lines run from 4.30am and begin their last journey at around 11.30pm.

The HÉV suburban train line, which runs on five lines (north from Batthyány tér in Buda via Óbuda and Aquincum to

Szentendre, south to both Csepel and Ráckeve, and east to Gödöllő), is almost like a fifth, above-ground metro line. Lines are designated H5 to H9.

Bus

An extensive system of buses running on some 268 routes day and night serves greater Budapest. On certain bus lines the same bus may have an 'E' after the number, meaning it is express and makes limited stops.

Buses run from around 4.30am to between 9pm and 11.50pm, depending on the line. From 11.50pm to 4.30am a network of 40 night buses (always with three digits and beginning with 9) operates every 15 to 60 minutes, again depending on the route.

The following are bus routes (shown with blue lines on most Budapest maps) that you might find useful:

7 Cuts across a large swath of central Pest from XIV Bosnyák tér and down VII Rákóczi út before crossing Elizabeth Bridge to southern Buda. The 7E makes limited stops on the same route.

15 Takes in most of the Inner Town from IX Boráros tér to XIII Lehel tér north of Nyugati train station.

105 Goes from V Deák Ferenc tér to XII Apor Vilmos tér in central Buda.

Tram

Trams are often faster and generally more pleasant for sightseeing than buses. There are 32 lines in total.

Some important tram lines (always marked with a red line on a Budapest map):

2 Scenic tram that travels along the Pest side of the Danube from V Jászai Mari tér to IX Boráros tér and beyond.

4 and 6 Extremely useful trams that start at XI Fehérvári út and XI Móricz Zsigmond körtér in south Buda, respectively, and follow the entire length of the Big Ring Rd in Pest before terminating at II Széll Kálmán tér in Buda. Tram 6 runs every 10 to 15 minutes round the clock.

19 Runs from southern Buda along XI Bartók Béla út through the Tabán and along the Danube to I Batthyány tér.

47, 48 and 49 Link V Deák Ferenc tér in Pest with points in southern Buda via the Little Ring Road.

61 Connects XI Móricz Zsigmond körtér with Déli train station and II Széll Kálmán tér in Buda.

Taxi

Taxis in Budapest are cheap by European standards, and are – at long last – fully regulated, with uniform flagfall (700Ft) and per-kilometre charges (300Ft). Waiting time is 75Ft per minute.

Be careful when hailing a taxi on the street, though. Avoid at all costs 'taxis' with no name on the door. Never get into a taxi that does not have a yellow licence plate and an identification badge displayed on the dashboard (as required by law), plus the logo of one of the reputable taxi firms on the outside of the side doors and a table of fares clearly visible on the right-side back door.

Reputable taxi firms:

Budapest Taxi (☎1-777 7777; www.budapesttaxi.hu)

City Taxi (☎1-211 1111; www.citytaxi.hu)

Fő Taxi (☎1-222 2222; www.fotaxi.hu)

Taxi 4 (☎1-444 4444; www.taxi4.hu)

Essential Information

Accessible Travel

Budapest has taken great strides in recent years in making public areas and facilities more accessible to the disabled. Wheelchair ramps, toilets fitted for those with disabilities and inward-opening doors, though not as common as in Western Europe, do exist. Audible traffic signals for the blind are commonplace, as are Braille plates in public lifts.

Hungarian Federation of Disabled Persons' Associations (MEOSZ; ☎1-388 2387; www.meosz.hu; III San Marco utca 76) Travellers with disabilities who are seeking information can contact this umbrella group.

Download Lonely Planet's free Accessible Travel guide from http://lptravel.to/AccessibleTravel.

Business Hours

Banks 7.45am or 8am to 5pm Monday to Thursday, to between 2pm and 4pm Friday

Bars 11am to midnight Sunday to Thursday, to 2am Friday and Saturday

Businesses 9am or 10am to 6pm Monday to Friday, to 1pm or 2pm Saturday

Clubs 4pm to 2am Sunday to Thursday, to 4am Friday and Saturday; some weekends only

Grocery stores and supermarkets 7am to 7pm Monday to Friday, to 3pm Saturday; some also to noon Sunday

Restaurants 11am to 11pm; breakfast venues open by 8am

Shops 10am to 6pm Monday to Friday, to 1pm Saturday

Discount Cards

Budapest Card (www.budapestinfo.hu; per 24/48/72/96/120hr 6490/9990/12,990/15,990/18,900Ft) Free admission to selected museums and other sights in and around the city; unlimited travel on all forms of public transport; two free guided walking tours; and discounts for organised tours, car rental, thermal baths, and at selected shops and restaurants. Available at tourist offices but cheaper online.

Electricity

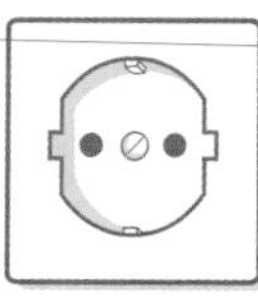

Type F
230V/50Hz

Emergencies

Ambulance ☎104

Fire ☎105

General Emergency ☎112

Police ☎107

Money

Currency Hungary's currency is the forint (Ft). Many hotels state prices in euros.

ATMs Everywhere.

Credit Cards Widely accepted everywhere.

Changing Money Avoid moneychangers (especially those on V Váci utca) in favour of banks.

Tipping Tipping is widely practised.

Money-Saving Tip

If you are using public transport a lot, make life easier (and safer) and buy a pass. It saves fiddling for a new ticket each time, keeps you safe from inspectors and almost always works out cheaper.

In restaurants, for decent service tip 10–15%. Never leave money on the table; instead, tell waiters how much you intend to leave and they will give the change accordingly. For taxis, you can just round up the fare.

Public Holidays

Hungary celebrates 10 *ünnep* (holidays) each year.

New Year's Day 1 January

National Day 15 March

Easter Monday March/April

Labour Day 1 May

Whit Monday May/June

St Stephen's Day 20 August

1956 Remembrance Day/Republic Day 23 October

All Saints' Day 1 November

Christmas holidays 25 and 26 December

Safe Travel

- Don't even think about riding 'black' (without paying a fare) on any public transport in Budapest because you *will* be caught and heavily fined.
- Taxis are much more regulated now but avoid the 'freelancers' with no company name on the door; these are just guys with cars (though licensed) and more likely to rip you off.
- Excessive billing of customers still occasionally happens in some bars and restaurants, so make sure to check your bill carefully.
- Pickpocketing is quite common in busy public places.

Telephone Services

- For local calls, dial the number (seven digits in Budapest, six elsewhere).
- All localities in Hungary have a two-digit area code, except for Budapest, which has just a ☎1.
- You must always dial ☎06 when ringing mobile phones, which have specific area codes depending on the company.

Toilets

- Public toilets in Budapest are relatively common but often in poor condition.
- A fee of 200Ft to 300Ft is typically payable.
- Toilets in restaurants and shopping malls are always a better bet.

Tourist Information

The **Budapest Info** (☎1-576 1401; www.budapestinfo.hu; V Sütő utca 2; ⏰8am-8pm; Ⓜ M1/2/3 Deák Ferenc tér, 🚊47, 49) office that is located near Deák Ferenc tér is probably the best single source of information about Budapest. This office stocks information about attractions and has purchasable maps; it can be crowded in summer.

Dos & Don'ts

Hungarians are almost always extremely polite in their social interactions, and the language can be very courtly – even when doing business with the butcher or having one's hair cut.

Greetings Young people's standard greeting to their elders is *Csókolom* ('I kiss it' – 'it' being the hand, of course). People of all ages, even close friends, shake hands when meeting up.

Asking for help Say *legyen szíves* ('be so kind as') to attract attention; say *bocsánat* ('sorry') to apologise.

Eating and drinking If you're invited to someone's home, bring a bunch of flowers or a bottle of good local wine.

Name days As much as their birthday, Hungarians celebrate their name day, which is usually the Catholic feast day of their patron saint (Hungarian calendars list them). Flowers, sweets or wine are the usual gifts.

Visas

- Citizens of European countries as well as Australia, Canada, Israel, Japan, New Zealand and the USA don't need visas for visits of up to 90 days.
- Check the current visa requirements that are listed on the website of the Ministry of Foreign Affairs (http://konzuliszolgalat.kormany.hu).

Language

Hungarian is a member of the Finno-Ugric language family; it is related very distantly to Finnish and Estonian. There are approximately 14.5 million speakers of Hungarian.

To enhance your trip with a phrasebook, visit **lonelyplanet.com**. Lonely Planet iPhone phrasebooks are available via the Apple App store.

Basics

Hello. (singular/plural)
Szervusz. — *ser*·vus
Szervusztok. — *ser*·vus·tawk

Goodbye.
Viszontlátásra — *vi*·sawnt·laa·taash·ro.

Yes./No.
Igen./Nem. — *i*·gen/nem

Please. (pol/inf)
Kérem. — *kay*·rem

Thank you.
Köszönöm. — *keu*·seu·neum

You're welcome.
Szívesen. — see·ve·shen

Excuse me.
Elnézést kérek. — *el*·nay·zaysht *kay*·rek

Sorry.
Sajnálom. — *shoy*·naa·lawm

How are you?
Hogy van — hawd' von

Fine. And you?
Jól. És Ön? — yāwl aysh eun

Do you speak English?
Beszél angolul? — *be*·sayl *on*·gaw·lul

I don't understand.
Nem értem. — nem *ayr*·tem

Eating & Drinking

The menu, please.
Az étlapot, kérem. — az *ayt*·lo·pawt *kay*·rem

I'd like a local speciality.
Valamilyen helyi specialitást szeretnék. — *vo*·lo·mi·yen *he*·yi *shpe*·tsi·o·li·taasht *se*·ret·nayk

What would you recommend?
Mit ajánlana? — *mit o*·yaan·lo·no

Do you have vegetarian food?
Vannak önöknél vegetáriánus ételek? — *von*·nok *eu*·neuk·nayl *ve*·ge·taa·ri·aa·nush *ay*·te·lek

I'd like..., please.
Legyen szíves, hozzon egy... — *le*·dyen *see*·vesh *hawz*·zawn ej...

Cheers! (to one person)
Egészségére! — *e*·gays·shay·gay·re

Cheers! (to more than one person)
Egészségükre! — *e*·gays·shay·gewk·re

That was delicious!
Ez nagyon finom volt! — ez *no*·dyawn *fi*·nawm vawlt

Please bring the bill.
Kérem, hozza a számlát. — *kay*·rem *hawz*·zo o *saam*·laat

Shopping

I want to buy ...
Szeretnék venni ... — *se*·ret·nayk *ven*·ni ...

I'm just looking.
Csak nézegetek. chok *nay*·ze·ge·tek

Can I look at it?
Megnézhetem? *meg*·nayz·he·tem

How much is this?
Mennyibe kerül ez? *men'*·yi·be *ke*·rewl ez

That's too expensive.
Ez túl drága. ez tūl *draa*·go

There's a mistake in the bill.
Valami hiba van a számlában. *vo*·lo·mi *hi*·bo von o *saam*·laa·bon

Emergencies

Help!
Segítség! *she*·geet·shayg

Go away!
Menjen el! *men*·yen el

Call the police!
Hívja a rendőrséget! *heev*·yo o *rend*·ēūr·shay·get

Call a doctor!
Hívjon orvost! *heev*·yawn *awr*·vawsht

I'm lost.
Eltévedtem. *el*·tay·ved·tem

I'm sick.
Rosszul vagyok. *raws*·sul vo·dyawk

Where are the toilets?
Hol a véce? hawl o *vay*·tse

Time & Numbers

What time is it?
Hány óra? haan' *āw*·ra

It's (one/10) o'clock.
(Egy/Tíz) óra van. (ed'/teez) *āw*·ra von

morning	*reggel*	*reg*·gel
afternoon	*délután*	*dayl*·u·taan
evening	*este*	*esh*·te
yesterday	*tegnap*	*teg*·nop
today	*ma*	mo
tomorrow	*holnap*	*hawl*·nop

1	*egy*	ed'
2	*kettő*	*ket*·tēū
3	*három*	*haa*·rawm
4	*négy*	nayd'
5	*öt*	eut
6	*hat*	hot
7	*hét*	hayt
8	*nyolc*	nyawlts
9	*kilenc*	*ki*·lents
10	*tíz*	teez
100	*száz*	saaz
1000	*ezer*	e·zer

Transport & Directions

Where's (the market)?
Hol van (a piac)? hawl von (o *pi*·ots)

What's the address?
Mi a cím? mi o tseem

Can you show me (on the map)?
Meg tudja mutatni nekem (a térképen)? meg *tud*·yo *mu*·tot·ni *ne*·kem (o *tayr*·kay·pen)

Does it stop at (Parliament)?
Megáll (Parlamenthez) on? *meg*·aall (*por*·lo·ment·hez) on

What time does it leave?
Mikor indul? *mi*·kawr *in*·dul

Please stop here.
Kérem, álljon meg itt. *kay*·rem *aall*·yawn meg itt

Is this taxi available?
Szabad ez a taxi? *so*·bod ez o *tok*·si

Behind the Scenes

Send Us Your Feedback

We love to hear from travellers – your comments help make our books better. We read every word, and we guarantee that your feedback goes straight to the authors. Visit **lonelyplanet.com/contact** to submit your updates and suggestions.

Note: We may edit, reproduce and incorporate your comments in Lonely Planet products such as guidebooks, websites and digital products, so let us know if you don't want your comments reproduced or your name acknowledged. For a copy of our privacy policy visit lonelyplanet.com/privacy.

Steve's Thanks

Thanks to Virág Katona, Judit Maróthy, Dávid Máté, Ildikó Nagy Moran, Bea Szirti and Adrian Zador for their very helpful suggestions. Gábor Banfalvi and Péter Lengyel showed me the correct wine roads to follow; Tony Láng and Balázs Váradi the political ones. Once again Michael Buurman opened his flat; thanks to Tal Lev for hospitality. *Nagyon szépen köszönöm mindenkinek!* As always, I'd like to dedicate my share of this to partner Michael Rothschild, with love and gratitude.

Acknowledgements

Cover photograph: Castle Hill, Budapest, Atlantide Phototravel/ Getty ©

Photographs pp28–9 (clockwise from top right): photo.ua/Shutterstock ©, posztos/Shutterstock ©, waku/Shutterstock ©.

This Book

This 3rd edition of Lonely Planet's *Pocket Budapest* guidebook was researched and written by Steve Fallon. This guidebook was produced by the following:

Destination Editor Brana Vladisavljevic

Senior Product Editor Elizabeth Jones

Product Editor Alison Ridgway

Senior Cartographer Valentina Kremenchutskaya

Book Designer Wibowo Rusli

Assisting Editors Janet Austin, Bruce Evans, Rosie Nicholson, Monique Perrin

Assisting Cartographers Katerina Pavkova

Cover Researcher Naomi Parker

Thanks to Josephine Blaazer, Philip Dunn, Shona Gray, Niamh O'Brien, Jeremy Parkinson, Lesley Shayler

Index

See also separate subindexes for:
Eating p157
Drinking p158
Entertainment p159
Shopping p159

Sights 000
Map Pages **000**

Sights 000
Map Pages **000**

Eating

Drinking

Sights 000
Map Pages **000**